Helping Teachers Manage Classrooms

Daniel L. Duke, editor

Association for Supervision
and Curriculum Development
225 North Washington Street
Alexandria, Virginia 22314

Editing:
    Ronald S. Brandt, ASCD Executive Editor
    Nancy Carter Modrak, Managing Editor, Booklets

Cover design:
    Al Way, Art Director

ISBN: 0-87120-113-5
Stock number: 611-82266
Library of Congress Card Catalog Number: 82-70273

Contents

Foreword

S OME circumstances of schooling will not disappear. They cannot be wished away or researched away or administered away. They can be obscured for a time with fresh slogans, but such laundering never really works. Easy nostrums can grab attention from the complexities of classroom reality and even may be associated with a feeling that at long last the problems are being attacked. Such superficial panaceas, with their arrogant titles, never seem to linger; like fireflies in the night, they are noted briefly and remembered even less.

Discipline is one of these hardy, tenacious concerns. We know it is discipline, even though we change its name, and we recognize that we need help as we seek understanding of both our pupils and ourselves. As we try each proposed solution, we know that solution is temporary at best. We want administrative support in both policy and action. We want collegial and parental understanding and support. We teachers want to teach, and discipline—or classroom management—consumes precious time and energy.

Assistance on classroom management is available. This ASCD booklet can help, but it is not a remedy. It is neither panacea nor bandage. It does not consist of classroom folklore or homilies. Rather, it presents substantial evidence and thoughtful conclusions sifted from abundant research and considered action in thousands of real classrooms.

To be most useful, this booklet must be read, thought about, and talked about. It can stimulate discussion among faculty colleagues; it can be a ready reference for individual teachers as well as a source for fruitful dialogue on school policy formation and personal development. As good as this booklet is—and it does represent well the very best recent scholarship on classroom management—it does not consider every important principle. Its suggestions are absolutely practical because they derive from the practice of experienced teachers. Yet its discussion must be considered thought-fully.

For instance, I would like to know better than I now do what my colleagues and pupils understand from the term classroom management. Is it a slightly more palatable cover for the harsher sounding and more familiar term "discipline"? How do my colleagues and I understand the implicit assumption of "control"? Also, what is the greater goal of class-room management? Maybe some people mean only a quiet and orderly classroom. Does that goal mean more academic on-task learner behavior and decreased teacher frustration in conducting instruction? We should consider such questions, debate them, and in the process penetrate more deeply into our own personal meanings.

Our greater intent in classroom management is to foster pupils' development of their own discipline, their own self-control, their own self-understanding. External control, by whatever name, by itself seems unlikely to yield such outcomes. Yet, control that is informed and informative and shared seems reasonable. To impose, monitor, and enforce rules is patently inadequate and incomplete in schools of a democracy. Rule development and observance, with adequate attention to consequences, is likely to aid both classroom deportment and personal development. For a teacher and a class of students to live together month after month, time off from academic tasks is required. Much "on-task" time must be allotted to living and working together toward a worthy goal.

We thank Daniel L. Duke and his colleagues for their work on this volume. Theirs is not the translation of research into practice. Rather, they have revealed the power of practice and have generated thoughtful ap-proaches to help us deal once again with one of schooling's most persistent concerns.

O. L. DAVIS
President, 1982-83
Association for Supervision and
Curriculum Development

Introduction:

Let's Look at Classroom Management

Problems of discipline and self-control assume a new significance and realism in today's world. In a complex civilization, the individual often has to subjugate his personal inclinations, whims, comforts, even some of his liberties to bigger goals than personal ones.

So began the opening section of *Discipline for Today's Children and Youth,* the first effort by the Association for Supervision and Curriculum Development to address the perennial problem of student conduct. Written in 1944 by George V. Sheviakov and Fritz Redl, that small and wonderfully practical volume went through 30 reprints before being revised in 1956 by Sybil K. Richardson.

Since the 40s and 50s, many changes have occurred in American society. The wartime emphasis on self-sacrifice and the common good gave way to what social critic Christopher Lasch dubbed a culture of narcissism. Steadily escalating expectations, the desire for immediate gratification, and the erosion of the "work ethic" characterize much of contemporary life. Public education has not escaped change. Various groups demand their rightful share of schooling's benefits. The courts and the government are asked to intervene more frequently to protect the interests of young people. Educators no longer enjoy the broad discretionary authority of surrogate parents.

The growing complexity of the job of teaching is reflected in changes in terminology. Sheviakov and Redl wrote about "discipline." "Classroom management" now constitutes a more descriptive term. As defined in the preface to the 1979 Yearbook of the National Society for the Study of Education, a volume entitled *Classroom Management,* the term encompasses "the provisions and procedures necessary to establish and maintain an environment in which instruction and learning can occur." The critical element of the teacher's role thus shifts from control to management—management of time, space, materials, auxiliary personnel, and students.

Changes in the conceptualization of the teacher's role obviously have implications for those who work with teachers—administrators, staff developers, curriculum specialists, and teacher educators. As of 1981, however, none of the dozens of volumes devoted to classroom management have been written expressly for these individuals. At the behest of Ron Brandt of ASCD, a group of educators met at Stanford University in the summer of 1980 to formulate a book that might speak to this audience. The participants in that meeting included many of the foremost authorities on the subject of classroom management: Lyn Corno, Carolyn Evertson, Paul Gump, Adrienne Meckel, Mary Rohrkemper, William Seidman, Beverly Showers, Robert Spaulding, Jane Stallings, and Gail Von Huene. The present volume represents, in large measure, the fruits of their labors.

Each of the eight chapters has been specially written for this book and each says something important to those who work with teachers.

In the opening section, entitled "What It Takes To Be An Effective Classroom Manager," researchers report on recent studies of teacher behaviors associated with orderly, productive instruction. Carolyn Evertson and Edmund Emmer, from the University of Texas at Austin, describe strategies for preventing student behavior problems. Jere Brophy, of the Institute for Research on Teaching at Michigan State University, next draws an important distinction between group management techniques and strategies for dealing with individual students who experience exceptional difficulties in class. Vernon Jones, Professor of Education at Lewis and Clark College, concludes the section with an analysis of the types of teacher training necessary to provide schools with effective classroom managers.

"Getting Help" is the focus of the second section. Phil C. Robinson, a Detroit principal, and Gail Von Huene, a staff development specialist with California's Master Plan, review some of the many sources of assistance available to teachers faced with classroom management difficulties. Pursuing a somewhat different tack, Mary Rohrkemper, of the University of Maryland, looks at ways teachers can assess their own behavior and embark on a systematic course of self-improvement.

The concluding section, "Classroom Management in Context," covers some of the less obvious dimensions of maintaining order in schools. Paul Gump, of the University of Kansas and one of the senior researchers in the field of classroom management, proposes a way to help educators better understand how the structure of groups can contribute to behavior problems. Succeeding chapters by William Wayson and Gay Su Pinnell (Ohio State University) and William Seidman (Stanford University) and myself go one step beyond groups to investigate the ways in which aspects of school organization influence student behavior and teacher efforts to deal with it.

It is the sincere hope of all the authors that the material in the following pages will prove of value to all those committed to . . . helping teachers manage classrooms.

DANIEL L. DUKE
Director, Educational Administration Program
Lewis and Clark College

Part One: What It Takes To Be An Effective Classroom Manager

1

Preventive Classroom Management

Carolyn M. Evertson and Edmund T. Emmer

W<small>E</small> present in this chapter the strategies and processes that teachers can use to establish well-managed classrooms. Although we stress the importance of planning and implementing key management features early in the school year, we also give attention to maintaining the system throughout the year. Our recommendations are based on two year-long descriptive studies of management methods. In the first study, we observed 27 third-grade teachers both at the beginning and throughout the school year. We followed the same observation schedule in a second study, which involved identifying management methods and their effects in 51 seventh- and eighth-grade English and mathematics teachers' classrooms. Both studies were conducted in a large Southwestern school system serving approximately 60,000 students having a tri-ethnic and varying socioeconomic composition. The third-grade study was conducted in eight schools, four of which were eligible for Title I programs. The junior high study included classrooms in all 11 of the district's junior high schools. The observed classroom practices of effective teachers are the basis for the management concepts and principles we present in this chapter.

Our presentation of key concepts begins with an overview of criteria for effective classroom management and a brief description of the research results upon which our management recommendations are based. Following that, we offer a series of suggestions for achieving good management. Although we present a fairly extensive treatment of major dimensions of management effectiveness, the reader should realize that we have not included all aspects. For example, we do not specifically discuss room arrangement and the management of highly heterogeneous or very low achieving classes (although many of our recommendations do apply to these contexts). Likewise, we have not developed the concept of teacher sensitivity or receptivity to student input, a characteristic of many of our better managers. Our choice of material for inclusion in the chapter was dictated by considerations of length needed for adequate coverage, amenability to presentation in this form, and wide applicability to a variety of contexts.

Our conception of management is not revolutionary and startling. Many of the management features we describe will be familiar to the reader who has had extensive experience in classrooms. Nevertheless, we hope that such a reader will find the conceptions of management to be useful: first, as an aid in identifying critical management tasks and technical skills; second, as a basis for communicating with less experienced teachers or teachers having management problems; lastly, perhaps as confirmation for the reader's own observations and intuitions.

A discussion of classroom management can profitably begin with a consideration of the goals or purposes of the management function. One major goal for management is establishing a climate for learning. A management system that interferes with student learning is unacceptable no matter what its other virtues might be. However, management behaviors are an indirect—rather than direct—cause of student learning. That is, management influences other features of the classroom, behavior, or instruction which are more direct causes of learning. However, ineffective management might directly impede learning by causing student behavior that is incompatible with attention or comprehension. Thus, an operational goal for the teacher's management system, related to creating a climate for learning, is to promote the development of high levels of engagement in academic tasks, and to prevent widespread disruptive or other off-task behaviors. As Dunkin and Biddle (1974) put it, ". . . it seems to us that adequate management of the classroom environment also forms a necessary condition for cognitive learnings; and if the teacher cannot solve problems in this sphere, we can give the rest of teaching away" (p. 135).

Another goal of the management function derives from a consideration of the task faced by the teacher in organizing instruction and activities for large groups of children. The teacher's goals must embrace both custody and socialization of children, as well as learning and evaluation concerns. Lortie (1975) has succinctly captured the essence of the teacher's task:

The teacher . . . is expected to elicit work from students. Students in all subjects and activities must engage in directed activities which are believed to produce learning. Their behavior, in short, should be purposeful, normatively controlled, and steady; concerns with discipline and control, in fact, largely revolve around the need to get work done by immature, changeful, and divergent persons who are confined in a small space (p. 151).

Thus, a major management goal, which is both immediate and continuously present, is to engage students in school work and to keep them engaged. Depending on the age of the students and their ability to remain involved in classroom tasks, teachers must provide enough variety of activities or tasks to maintain attention. In addition, teachers must socialize students to the classroom setting and, except for certain activities that take place outside the classroom, accept responsibility for the custody of all the students throughout the day. Therefore, the school and classroom setting and their associated institutional roles impose on teachers management goals that are not necessarily related to learning goals.

It is not surprising that instructional approaches (for example, an individual diagnostic-prescriptive method) that run counter to some of the constraints imposed by school and classroom setting characteristics, are not easily used, or if they are used, are greatly modified. An appreciation for how the characteristics of a setting might influence classroom processes and behaviors, whose ostensible goal is promotion of student learning, can be gained by considering a noneducational example. Imagine how a pediatrician's task would be changed if, at 8:00 a.m. he or she was greeted by 30 children with assorted disorders in a single room from which no one was allowed to leave until 3:00 p.m. except for lunch.

Effective management therefore must take into account both long-range goals for student learning and short-range goals of maintaining task involvement. In addition, management tasks must be appropriate for the settings and activities of schools and classrooms. If management strategies are to succeed, they must "fit" their context.

Recognizing Effective Management

In order to derive principles of classroom management from existing classroom practices, it is necessary first to be able to recognize effective management. One way to proceed is to define student behaviors that indicate an effective management system is in place and then to identify what teachers do to obtain these positive indicators.

The following vignettes illustrate several features of classrooms differing in management effectiveness, which is essentially defined in terms of a high degree of student involvement and participation in the academic tasks of the classroom, and minimal amounts of disruptive or other off-task student behaviors. Each example takes place in an elementary school classroom during the middle of a morning.

One of the reading groups has just completed an oral reading and recitation session. The children leave the group area and quietly return to their seats, where they take out their notebooks and begin a seatwork activity. After a few minutes of checking student progress, the teacher calls for another group of children who moves to the group area without interrupting other children. While the teacher works with this group, the remainder of the class continues with the seatwork assignments. When children complete their activity, they get out a spelling book or resume working on an activity they had begun earlier. Some children work together, conducting a drill over the spelling words. Some whisper quietly, although the noise level does not interfere with other students or the teacher. When pupils are out of their seats, it is only to perform necessary tasks. Their off-task behaviors are brief, more like rest periods than prolonged avoidance of work. When the teacher calls for papers later in the morning, all the children hand in completed work.

We can infer that the class is well managed because the students exhibited a high level of involvement in all the activities, and cooperated with both the teacher and each other in accomplishing tasks. Important routines, such as what to do when finished with an assignment, were in effect. Finally, there was no evidence of disruptive or inappropriate behavior.

Consider a second example.

While the teacher is working with a reading group, several out-of-group children wander around the classroom. Other children come up to the teacher with questions, interrupting group time. When the teacher finishes with the group, the children take several minutes to return to their seats to begin the next activity. The teacher does not notice the numerous children who are avoiding work, because she is involved with helping two children get started on a ditto handout. When the teacher resumes work with another reading group, loud noises and commotion cause her to interrupt the group activity in order to restore order in the class. The attentiveness of children in the group wanes as they are distracted throughout by the noise and interruptions. Eventually, the teacher extends the reading activities into the period scheduled for spelling, causing the latter activity to be shortened. When the seatwork papers are called for, less than half the class has completed them.

The preceding example illustrates several indicators of poor management. Many of the children avoided responsibility for work during the morning's activities. Some children interfered with the teacher's small-group work, and inappropriate behavior was frequent. Some important procedures—such as what to do when help is needed and the teacher is busy—were not working. Finally, the teacher was diverted from the planned schedule so that instruction in one of the language arts was lost.

These examples illustrate some of the major criteria with which we define good classroom management. Effective management consists of those teacher behaviors that produce high levels of student involvement in classroom activities and minimize student behaviors that interfere with the teacher's or other students' work and efficient use of instructional time.

Student behavior criteria are also observable and, to a considerable extent, are the result of differences in management systems in classrooms. These student behaviors, however, are short-term criteria for management effectiveness and derive chiefly from the teacher's goal of engaging children in relevant work. But is there any evidence that such criteria are related to the longer range goals of academic achievement? The answer to this question appears to be yes.

Research on the relationship between student involvement and achievement has been reviewed by Jackson (1968) and Bloom (1976). They found consistent evidence in numerous studies of a positive relationship, both at the individual student level and at the class level, between student involvement or attention and achievement. Recent reviews of the process-product research literature have also highlighted the importance of classroom management variables in predicting student achievement gain (Brophy, 1979; Good, 1979; Medley, 1977). In our own research, we have also found a positive relationship. It should be noted, though, that the magnitude of relationship in the research literature is moderate, rather than high. That is, management is by no means the only explanatory variable for student achievement. The consistency with which this relationship has been found does support its being an enabling characteristic allowing good instruction to have positive effects on achievement.

Two Studies of Classroom Management and Organization

The strategies and processes for well-managed classrooms that we recommend are based on our findings in two studies we conducted for the Classroom Organization and Effective Teaching Project at the University of Texas' Research and Development Center for Teacher Education in Austin.[1]

---

[1] Research reported in this chapter was supported in part by the National Institute of Education, Contract No. OB-NIE-G-80-0116, P2, The Classroom Organization and Effective Teaching Project, Research and Development Center for Teacher Education, The University of Texas at Austin. The opinions expressed do not necessarily reflect the position or policy of the National Institute of Education and no official endorsement by that office should be inferred.

Third-Grade Classrooms

The primary focus of the first study, conducted in 27 self-contained third-grade classrooms, was to determine how teachers organized and managed their classes beginning with the first day of school. Our objectives were:

(a) to learn what principles of organization and management are most important at the beginning of the year and which are most important for maintaining effective classroom management throughout the year;

(b) to collect a large body of very specific examples of management skills and techniques to illustrate these general principles;

(c) to develop methodology that contained both qualitative and quantitative observation techniques in order to provide a rich but objective view of classrooms.

The 27 classes in this study were located in eight schools in a large urban school district. Each class was observed eight or nine times during the first three weeks of school. Each observation lasted from two to four hours, resulting in an average of 25 hours of observations for each class. Observations during the remainder of the year were obtained at roughly three-week intervals. We used a variety of instruments to record and classify behavior, including narrative records, student engagement rates, and component ratings.

Observers in the study were trained to take narrative records describing in detail events relating to organization and management in the classrooms. These narratives preserved a chronology of events, while providing information about a large number of specific aspects. Observers also assessed student engagement at 15-minute intervals, counting the frequency of children who were on and off task in different activities. Student engagement was considered an important short-term outcome because of the research indicating that active on-task engagement is related to longer-term outcomes such as achievement. Observers also filled out a set of component ratings after each observation. These ratings were assessments of procedural clarity, use of materials, appropriate and inappropriate student behavior, and various other aspects of classroom organization and management. These assessments were made on five-point scales.

Numerous analyses were performed using the data collected throughout the year. For example, using case study methods, we made intensive analyses of highly effective classroom managers. Also, after matching classrooms on students' entering achievement levels, subgroups of effective and less effective classroom managers were identified. Selection criteria included student achievement gains as well as the rate of student engagement, the amount of inappropriate and disruptive behavior, and the average amount of off-task, unsanctioned behavior. The results of both qualitative and quantitative comparisons of the management behaviors of more or less effective teachers indicate several important differentiating characteristics: [2]

1. *Analyzing classroom tasks.* Better managers demonstrated an ability to analyze the tasks of the first few weeks of school in precise detail. Their presentations to the students about rules, procedures, and assignments were very clear, and they provided specific feedback to students when inappropriate behavior occurred. Thus, these teachers seemed to have a better behavioral map of the classroom and what was required for students to function within it.

2. *Teaching the going-to-school skills.* Better managers incorporated the teaching of rules and procedures as a very important part of instruction during the first few weeks. That is, they taught going-to-school skills by providing practice and moving through procedures, giving feedback, responding to signals, and pointing out to students when they were behaving appropriately.

3. *Seeing the classroom from the student's perspective.* Better organized teachers were able to see through the eyes of their students in planning the classroom and in introducing the students to new routines during the year. They appeared to predict what would confuse or distract their students and what would be of immediate concern to them.

4. *Monitoring student behavior.* The more successful teachers monitored students closely during the first few weeks and dealt with problems immediately. They did not ignore deviations from classroom rules and procedures.

Junior High Classrooms

A second descriptive study was conducted at the junior high level in seventh- and eighth-grade mathematics and English classes. We expected the strategies, procedures, and constraints facing junior high school teachers to differ in some ways from the organizational demands facing teachers in elementary school classrooms.

In this study, 26 mathematics teachers and 25 English teachers were each observed in two classes. Classroom data were obtained from an

---

[2] For more detailed descriptions of the results of the study, see Emmer and others (1980) and Anderson and others (1980).

average of 14 one-hour observations per class, and each teacher was observed intensively during the first three weeks, including an observation in one class on the first, second, and fourth days of school. Each observation provided quantitative measures of student task engagement, assessments of teacher and student behavior, and detailed narrative records of classroom events. As in the elementary school study, subsamples of more and less effective teachers were identified using classroom data obtained after the first three weeks of school. Once identified, the two groups were compared on a variety of measures of classroom processes and behaviors observed during the first three weeks. In addition, intensive analyses of effective managers throughout the year were conducted. Major differences between good and poor management behaviors could be detected and were similar to the results from the elementary school study. The following clusters were found to differentiate these groups: [3]

1. *Instructing students in rules and procedures.* Even though all of the teachers had rules and procedures, the more effective managers had more complete systems and were more successful in teaching and installing rules and procedures. Better managers were more explicit about what was desirable behavior.

2. *Monitoring student compliance with rules.* The more effective teachers were rated as being more consistent in managing behavior. They were less likely to ignore disruptive behavior and were more likely to use the rules and procedures when giving feedback to students. In short, effective teachers noted and reacted to departures from acceptable classroom behavior.

3. *Developing student accountability for work.* More effective managers kept better track of student progress and completion of assignments. They had stronger and more detailed accountability systems.

4. *Communicating information.* Effective managers were more successful in presenting information clearly, in giving directions, and in stating objectives. They were better able to segment complex tasks and break them down into step-by-step procedures. They also were assessed as having more understanding of their students' learning skills than the less effective managers.

5. *Organizing instruction.* More effective managers wasted less time in their activities and had more on-task time.

---

[3] For further results of this study, see Evertson and others (1981), Evertson and Emmer (in press), and Sanford and Evertson (1981).

Profile of an Effective Classroom Manager

The results from the junior high study were not markedly different from those we obtained at the elementary level. The commonalities indicate that the effective classroom manager has a clear set of expectations about appropriate and inappropriate behavior at the beginning of the year and communicates them to students in a variety of ways. The better manager establishes routines and procedures to guide student behavior in a variety of classroom activities and takes considerable care in teaching the system to the students. Departures from expected behavior are generally dealt with promptly so that students receive feedback, and the consequences are clear and consistent. The teacher monitors student behavior carefully and, thus, is aware of small problems before they become big ones. Better managers are also better communicators and are able to explain, give directions, and communicate information effectively.

There were some differences between management functions in the elementary school and the junior high school setting, but they were more a matter of adjustment to the age level, subject, and type of classroom grouping than differences in qualitative principles. For example, all good managers have well worked-out procedures for guiding student behavior in a variety of activities. The exact nature of those procedures, however, is a function of the particular settings and activities in individual classrooms.

Suggestions For Effective Management

Our recommendations for developing an effective classroom management system are organized into three major areas: planning before the year begins, management during the first few weeks, and key behaviors needed to implement and maintain a management system. Although the use of these suggestions will help teachers manage their classrooms, we stress that these recommendations are not intended to be a total basis for teaching. Instructional decisions also must be informed by curricular, developmental, and cultural concerns for children and for society in general. However, such higher level concerns are unlikely to have much weight in the teacher's decision making and in the interactive classroom processes of teachers unless the more basic management concerns are first resolved. Thus, we hope these recommendations will enable teachers to cope successfully with management concerns so the other factors that should also influence decisions about teaching can assume their proper role.

Planning Before the Year Begins

The planning phase of classroom management has three major steps: (1) determining expected behaviors, (2) translating expectations into procedures and rules, and (3) identifying consequences.

Step 1: Determining expected student behaviors. One of the major characteristics of effective classroom managers is their ability to communicate a clear set of expectations about appropriate behavior to their students. This critical management task is far more complex than simply stating several rules about conduct. Although such rules can be useful, establishing clear expectations requires more time and effort because desirable behaviors frequently vary according to the classroom activity.

For example, activities such as seatwork, small-group work, and whole-class instruction require very different student behaviors. Seatwork requires that students be able to work independently, follow directions, get help when they are unable to work on their own, and know what to do if they complete their seatwork. Whole-class instruction requires students to sit and listen to the teacher or other students, answer questions when asked, wait their turn to respond, and, frequently, raise their hands when they wish to volunteer a response or to ask a question. Thus, stating a few rules for behavior will not be sufficient to guide student behavior during such disparate activities. Because students are not automatically aware of, nor do they practice the behavior appropriate for an activity, it is the teacher's responsibility to know what the necessary behaviors are and to communicate them to the students.

Once the behavior needed in a particular setting has been identified, the teacher can then decide whether a procedure or routine should be established to help bring about the behavior. For example, suppose a desirable behavior during whole-class activities is that children speak in turn. To facilitate this behavior, children can learn to raise their hands and wait to be called on before they speak.

Table 1 (pages 13-16) contains a list of major areas for which elementary school teachers need a clear set of expectations. These areas include the use of classroom facilities, space, other areas of the school, whole-class activities, seatwork, small groups, and some miscellaneous areas. Table 2 (pages 16-18) contains a similar list for the junior high school or middle school setting. Although the lists are differentiated by grade level, intermediate grade elementary teachers may find aspects of the junior high/middle school list to be applicable to their setting. Likewise, the junior high teacher might profit from considering procedures commonly used in elementary schools. The list in Table 2 is shorter because the junior high school/middle school teacher typically meets with different groups of students throughout the day and can use the same procedures with each group. The elementary school teacher must work with the same students in many more activities and is responsible for managing children in a variety of settings throughout the day. Consequently, the number of procedures the elementary school teacher must plan is considerably greater.

Both tables contain suggestions based on observations of effective classroom managers. However, these suggestions are meant as examples rather than prescriptions because different expectations or procedures can be used successfully for a given activity; the important thing is that the teacher have some reasonable expectation in these areas. In addition, all possible areas are not treated. For example individualized instruction, team teaching, and special programs are not included in the table. Therefore, if a teacher intends to use such instructional activities or organizational patterns, then it will be necessary to add to the list the desirable behaviors for their activities and settings.

Tables 1 and 2 can be used as a basis for planning the beginning of the year. Teachers should identify desirable behavior in each area and note what, if any, associated routine or procedure they intend to use. Expectations for appropriate behavior in the areas identified in Tables 1 and 2 should be used with due consideration given to the age and grade levels of the children to be taught. Teachers who will be instructing an age level they have not had much experience with should definitely discuss their expectations about appropriate behavior with experienced teachers or administrators. In addition to providing feedback about initial plans, these persons can often be the source of valuable suggestions for age appropriate procedures and routines.

During inservice training sessions we have found the list to be helpful as a way of organizing small-group discussions. Teachers frequently have developed effective procedures to deal with some of these areas and such ideas can then be shared with other teachers. The list can also be used in preservice teacher education by supervisors or cooperating teachers. Usually student teachers do not observe the beginning of the year and are not sufficiently aware of the many behavioral expectations that are established at that time. Furthermore, student teachers are often not aware of the classroom procedures and routines that are in place, and how they function in the overall management system in a classroom. These lists can be used as a basis for helping increase such awareness.

Table 1. Expectations and Procedures for the Elementary School Classroom

Area of Behavior	A Common Expectation or Procedure
A. Student use of classroom space and facilities	
1. Desks or tables and student storage space	Students are usually expected to keep these clean and neat. Some teachers set aside a particular period of time each week for students to clean out desks. Alternatively, straightening out materials could be a good end-of-day routine.
2. Learning centers/stations	Appropriate behavior at the center, access to the center, care of materials, and procedures for coming and going should be considered.
3. Shared materials, bookshelves, drawers, and cabinets	Access and use should be spelled out.
4. Teacher's desk and storage areas	Frequently these are off limits to students, except when the teacher's permission is given.
5. Drinking fountain, sink, pencil sharpener, and bathroom	Decide when and how these can be used. Most teachers prefer not to have lines waiting at any of these locations.
B. Procedures concerning other areas of the school	
1. Out-of-class bathrooms, drinking fountains, office, library, resource rooms	Appropriate student behavior needs to be identified. Procedures for students coming to and going from these areas should be decided upon.
2. Coming and going from the classroom	Students need to learn how to line up properly and how to pass through the halls correctly. Consider such things as the condition of the room before lining up, and whether talking is allowed.
3. Playground	Expectations need to be identified for coming from and going to the playground, safety and maintenance rules, and how to get students' attention for lining up or listening. Some teachers use a coach's whistle.
4. Lunchroom	Expectations for table manners, behavior, and noise level should be identified.
C. Procedures during whole class activities	
1. Student participation in class discussions	Many teachers require students to raise their hands to be called on before speaking during whole-class activities.
2. Student involvement and attention	Students are expected to listen to the person who is talking.
3. Assignments	Many teachers record assignments on a chalkboard or elsewhere, or have students copy the assignments in notebooks.

13

Table 1 (continued)

Area of Behavior	A Common Expectation or Procedure
4. Talk among students during seatwork	Some teachers require silence; others allow quiet talk (very soft whispering). Also, teachers sometimes use a cue or signal to let students know when the noise level is unacceptable. For example, a bell rung once means no more talking. Also needed are procedures for students working together, if this is to be allowed, and some procedure to enable students to contact the teacher if they need help. Typical procedures involve students raising hands when help is needed or, if the teacher is involved with other students or in group work, the use of classroom monitors.
5. Passing out books, supplies	Supplies that are frequently used can be passed out by a monitor. Students need to know what to do while they wait for their materials.
6. Students turning in work	Teachers frequently have a set of shelves or an area where students turn in assignments when they are finished. Alternatively, a special folder for each student may be kept.
7. Handing back assignments to students	Prompt return of corrected papers is desirable. Many teachers establish a set time of the day to do this. Students need to know what to do with the material when they receive it (place it in a notebook, or folder, or take it home).
8. Make-up work	Procedures are needed for helping students who have been absent as well as for communicating assignments that must be made up.
9. Out of seat policies	Students need to know when it is acceptable to be out of seat and when permission is needed.
10. What to do when seatwork is finished	Some teachers use extra credit assignments, enrichment activities, free reading, etc.
D. Procedures during reading groups or other small-group work	
1. Student movement into and out of group	These transitions should be brief, quiet, and nondisruptive to other students. Many teachers use a bell to signal movement from seatwork to small group. This works when there is a preset order that students know.
2. Bringing materials to the group	Students need to know what they are to bring with them to the group. One way to communicate this is to include a list of the materials along with posted assignments.

14

Table 1 (continued)

Area of Behavior	A Common Expectation or Procedure
3. Expected behavior of students in the group	Just as in whole-group activities, students need clear expectations about what behaviors are appropriate in small-group work.
4. Expected behavior of students not in the small group	Students out of the group also need clear expectations about desirable behavior. Important areas include noise level, student talk, access to the teacher, and what to do when the seatwork assignment or other activities are completed. Effective managers avoid problems by giving very clear instructions for activities of students out-of-group. Checking briefly between groups also helps prevent problems from continuing as well as allowing monitoring. Student helpers may also be identified.
E. Other procedures that must be decided upon	
1. Beginning the school day	Establishing a consistent routine, such as the Pledge of Allegiance, date, birthdays, and overview of the morning's activities, or passing back graded papers, helps start the day while still giving time for late arrivals and for administrative matters to be accomplished.
2. Administrative matters	Such details as attendance reporting, collecting lunch money, and other recordkeeping must be done while students are in the room. Teachers can set aside a specific time of the day for performing these tasks during which the students are expected to engage in some activity. For example, 10 minutes of quiet reading fills the time constructively while allowing the teacher to handle administrative tasks with little interruption.
3. End of school day	Routines can be planned for concluding each day. Straightening desks, gathering materials, singing a song, or reviewing activities and things learned during the day provide some structure for this major transition time.
4. Student conduct during interruptions and delays	Interruptions are inevitable and sometimes frequent. Students can be taught to continue working if interrupted, or to sit patiently and quietly otherwise.
5. Fire drills, and other precautionary measures	School procedures need to be identified and carefully taught to the children.

15

Table 1 (continued)

Area of Behavior	A Common Expectation or Procedure
6. Housekeeping and student helpers	Most children love to help, and the teacher need only identify specific tasks. They are also a good way to help some children learn responsibility. Some possibilities: feeding classroom pets, watering plants, erasing chalkboards, acting as line leader, messenger, etc. A procedure for choosing and rotating responsibilities among students needs to be established.

Note. This table is adapted from the manual, *Organizing and Managing the Elementary School Classroom,* Carolyn M. Evertson, Edmund T. Emmer, Barbara S. Clements, Julie P. Sanford, Murray E. Worsham, and Ellen L. Williams. Austin, Texas: The Research and Development Center for Teacher Education, The University of Texas at Austin, August 1980.

Table 2. Expectations and Procedures for Junior High School/Middle School Classrooms

Area of Behavior	A Common Expectation or Procedure
A. Procedures for beginning class	
1. Administrative matters	The teacher needs procedures to handle reporting absences and tardiness. Students need to know what behaviors are expected of them while the teacher is completing administrative procedures. Some teachers begin the period with a brief warm-up activity such as a few problems or a brief assignment. Others expect the students to sit quietly and wait for the teacher to complete the routine.
2. Student behavior before and at the beginning of the period	Procedures should be established for what students are expected to do when the tardy bell rings (be in seats, stop talking), behavior during PA announcements (no talking, no interruptions of the teacher), what materials are expected to be brought to class each day, and how materials to be used during the period will be distributed.
B. Procedures during whole-class instructional activities	
1. Student talk	Many teachers require that students raise their hands in order to receive permission to speak. Sometimes teachers allow chorus responses (everybody answers at once) without hand raising, but the teacher then needs to identify and use some signal to students which lets them know when such responding is appropriate.

Table 2 (continued)

Area of Behavior	A Common Expectation or Procedure
2. Use of the room by students	Students should know when it is appropriate to use the pencil sharpener, to obtain materials from shelves or bookcases, and if, and when, it is appropriate to leave their seats to seek help from the teacher or other students. Unclear expectations in this area result in some students spending time wandering about the room.
3. Leaving the room	Some procedure needs to be established for allowing students to use the bathroom, go to the library or school office, etc. Usually the school will have some specified system. We have noted that teachers who are free with hall passes frequently have large numbers of requests to leave the room.
4. Signals for attention	Frequently teachers use a verbal signal or a cue such as moving to a specific area of the room, ringing a bell, or turning on an overhead projector to signal to students. Such a signal, if used consistently, can be an effective device for making a transition between activities or for obtaining student attention.
5. Student behavior during seatwork	Expectations need to be established for what kind of talk, if any, may occur during seatwork, how students can get help, when out of seat behavior is or is not permitted, access to materials, and what to do if seatwork assignments are completed early.
6. Procedures for laboratory work or individual projects	A system for distributing materials when these are used is essential. Also, safety routines or rules are vital. Expectations regarding appropriate behavior should be established for students working individually or in groups, and when extensive movement around the room or coming and going is required. Finally, routines for cleaning up are suggested.
C. Expectations regarding student responsibility for work	
1. Policy regarding the form of work	Procedures can be established for how students are to place headings on paper, for the use of pen or pencil, and for neatness.
2. Policy regarding completion of assignments	The teacher will have to decide on whether incomplete or late work is acceptable, and under what conditions, and whether a penalty will be imposed. In addition, some procedure for informing students of due dates for assignments should be established, along with procedures for make-up work for students who were absent.

17

Table 2 (continued)

Area of Behavior	A Common Expectation or Procedure
3. Communicating assignments to students	An effective procedure for communicating assignments is to keep a list of each period's work assignments during a 2- or 3-week period of time. Posting this list allows students who were absent to easily identify necessary make-up work. Another useful procedure is to record the assignment for the day on an overhead projector transparency or on the front chalkboard, and require students to copy the assignment onto a piece of paper or into a notebook. Students who do not complete assignments in class will then have a record of what is expected when they return to the assignment at home or during a study period.
4. Checking procedures	Work that is to be checked by students in class can save the teacher time and provide quick feedback to students. Procedures should be established for exchanging papers, how errors are to be noted, and how papers are to be returned and passed to the teacher.
5. Grading policy	Students should know what components will be included in determining report card grades and the weight, or percent, of each component.
D. Other procedures	
1. Student use of teacher desk or storage areas	Generally these are kept off limits to students, except when the teacher gives special permission.
2. Fire and disaster drills	Students should be informed early in the year about what they are to do during such emergencies. Typically, the school will have a master plan and will conduct schoolwide drills.
3. Procedures for ending the class	Expectations regarding straightening up the room, returning to seats, noise level, and a signal for dismissal may be established. When cleanup requires more than a few seconds, teachers usually set aside the necessary time at the end of the period to complete the task before the bell rings.
4. Interruptions	Students need to know what is expected during interruptions (continue working, or sit quietly).

Note. This table is adapted from Tables 2 and 3 in the manual, *Organizing and Managing the Junior High Classroom*, Edmund T. Emmer, Carolyn M. Evertson, Barbara S. Clements, Julie P. Sanford, and Murray E. Worsham. Austin, Texas: The Research and Development Center for Teacher Education, The University of Texas at Austin, August 1981.

18

Step 2: Translating expectations into procedures and rules. After the teacher's expectations are identified it is helpful to translate them into procedures and rules. A procedure, or routine, is simply a behavior or series of behaviors that regularly occur at a specified time or during a particular activity. For activities that occur frequently, procedures should be identified to make efficient use of classroom time and to avoid confusion and delays. In contrast to classroom procedures, which typically specify the behavior in a particular activity or setting, classroom rules usually prescribe (or proscribe) behavior in general. The purpose of classroom rules is to call students' attention to the areas of behavior and to create a strong expectation about what is or is not acceptable. Some typical rules (the wording can be adapted to fit the grade level) include:

Be polite and helpful.
Respect your fellow students and adults.
No hitting, running, and shoving.
Raise your hand before speaking.
Keep your desk and the classroom clean and neat.
Listen when others speak.
Be in your seat when the bell rings.
Bring your materials every day.

These rules are only examples and are not meant to be a definitive list. Some teachers manage very well with only a few general classroom rules; others use more rules, some that prohibit certain behaviors they find objectionable or disruptive. Typically, the rules are posted somewhere in the classroom so that students can see them and the teacher can refer to them when necessary. Ideally, stated and posted rules function as cues to elicit appropriate behavior, or, in the case of a rule that prohibits certain behavior, to elicit a covert response inhibiting the inappropriate behavior.

In elementary classrooms, teachers frequently involve students in rule setting. In junior high school grades, teachers sometimes allow students to take part in rule setting but it is less frequently observed than in earlier grade levels. Perhaps its lower frequency at the junior high level is a function of the teacher's meeting with five different classes each day: if each class developed different rules, the teacher's management task would be unnecessarily complicated. Whether at the elementary or junior high level, the teacher should have a clear idea of the areas for which rules are needed before seeking student input, so that critical areas will not be overlooked in the discussion. In such a discussion of rules, students can be called on to identify reasons for rules, to suggest rules, or to provide specific examples for generally stated rules. If allowed, children will generate a long list of "don't" statements, so the teacher needs to skill-fully steer the discussion toward more positive, general statements.

Step 3: Identifying consequences. In this section we are concerned with student behaviors whose consequences are influenced by the teacher, bearing in mind that the teacher cannot influence *all* consequences. Plan-ning consequences enables the teacher to encourage appropriate behavior from the beginning of the year and to be in a position to act promptly to deal with inappropriate behavior when it occurs. Although children may follow rules and procedures simply because they have been asked to do so, eventually some incentive or reward is necessary to maintain co-operation. By planning consequences ahead of time, teachers increase the likelihood that they will use reasonable ones, and they avoid the incon-sistencies that occur when confronted by events for which they have no immediate response. While it is not possible to prepare for every eventu-ality in the classroom, it is possible to anticipate a substantial number of them.

The expectations for appropriate behavior and the associated rules and procedures from Steps 1 and 2 should be used systematically to plan consequences. Teachers can review their rules and procedures and con-sider a key question for each: What happens to students when they follow or fail to follow a procedure or rule? Generally speaking, positive con-sequences should follow appropriate behavior. However, teachers need not spend their time performing as "praise" machines, because conse-quences of appropriate behavior in classrooms are often naturally rein-forcing. Lining up correctly allows children to go to lunch or to recess; attention to a seatwork assignment brings about completion of the task; raising one's hand to volunteer often produces the opportunity to speak. Thus, a part of effective use of positive consequences is simply making certain that what is supposed to occur following appropriate behavior does in fact take place.

In addition to providing for naturally occurring consequences, teachers need to plan an additional incentive system. Such systems may range from very simple ones using mainly grades coupled with teacher attention and praise, to highly elaborate ones employing token economies, group contingencies, and individual contracts. The incentives available to teachers are wide-ranging and include praise, affection, Happy Faces, good grades, bonus points, a "good" note home, certificates and awards, a variety of tangible rewards obtained as a result of earning points or tokens, and a multitude of special privileges (for instance, being line leader, opportunity to play a special game, helper for the day, free read-ing time, and so forth). It is *not* necessary to have an elaborate incentive plan; we have seen effective managers use simple systems or complex systems. However, it is necessary to think through what incentives will be used for which behaviors; that is, what rules and procedures are especially critical to the management system. Such rules and procedures, along with behavior important to instructional functions, are good candidates for targets of the incentive system.

Careful attention must be paid to what will happen when students behave inappropriately. The teacher's response can range from imposing a penalty on an offending student (such as assigning detention for tardiness) to ignoring an unobtrusive and innocuous procedural violation (such as an inappropriate callout during a recitation). Handling inappropriate behavior well, and minimizing its recurrence, depends on careful consideration of what responses are available to the teacher and what is reasonable in the context in which the inappropriate behavior occurs. Teachers should review their procedures and rules and plan how they will manage deviations from them.

In some cases, particularly for major rule violations, some system of penalties will be needed. We do not wish to encourage punitive or repressive teacher behavior; however, some negative consequences appear to be necessary in order to deter behavior which, if unchecked, would soon lead to the disruption of normal classroom processes and to a poor learning environment. Commonly used penalties include detention, "time out" in a restricted area away from classmates, demerits or checks, sentences or some other repetitive activity (laps in physical education), and denying or withholding a privilege (loss of recess time, being last to leave the room at lunch, or losing "whispering" rights). When a check or demerit system is used, students receive a penalty (such as detention) after accumulating several demerits in a given period of time. In these cases, the first demerits serve as a warning. Such systems can be effective in helping students to learn to control their own behavior, but they require that the teacher have an efficient recordkeeping procedure. Many schools have schoolwide penalties for particular misbehaviors (detention for tardiness, suspension for fighting). In these instances, of course, teachers need to follow school procedures.

Penalties are useful in deterring students from violating major rules and repeatedly ignoring procedures. However, penalties are neither necessary nor desirable for most run-of-the-mill inappropriate behaviors that occur in classrooms. Too much time and energy will be consumed if the teacher frequently invokes penalties for minor violations; teachers should reserve penalties for major inappropriate behaviors.

Minor procedural violations—such as calling out, being out of seat, whispering to a neighbor, heading papers improperly, forgetting materials, pushing in line, leaving trash on the floor, and so on—should also have a consequence, but rarely would that consequence be a penalty. Unless these misbehaviors are continuous, consequences such as the following, which are simple to use and effective, should be sufficient:

1. Simply ask the child to stop the inappropriate behavior. Make sure the student knows what he or she is supposed to be doing, and then monitor until the inappropriate behavior ceases and the appropriate behavior begins.

2. Have the child repeat the procedure until it is performed correctly.

3. If several students perform a procedure inappropriately, reteach the procedure. Demonstrate it or have other students do it correctly.

If none of these techniques works, use a mild penalty. For example, withhold a privilege—students who do not line up properly leave the room last; incorrect form on an assignment or sloppy work results in loss of points, redoing the assignment, or a reduced grade; loud talkers lose the privilege of working together, and so on. A logical connection between the inappropriate behavior and its consequence helps students learn to avoid the inappropriate behavior.

Further discussion of incentive and penalty systems is beyond the scope of this chapter, but they have been extensively treated in the teacher education literature, and many good chapters and books are available.

Activities at the Beginning of the School Year

The first part of the school year is crucial in the classroom management cycle, for this is when children first encounter their teacher's expectations for their behavior and begin to learn how to behave in the new setting. A key goal during the first few weeks is to produce a pattern of learning-oriented behavior. Class norms should be established in favor of productive task engagement and cooperative behavior; disruptive behavior and other forms of off-task and inappropriate behavior should be minimized.

Although older students are more familiar with general expectations for appropriate behavior, for most students the novelty in the setting— new teachers, different books, more difficult content, different procedures, new classmates—makes them more receptive to acquiring new modes of responding or behaving. Thus, the time is ripe for teachers to use their role as classroom leader in order to present appropriate modes of behavior. Also, many students are anxious about school during the first few weeks of the new year. The teacher can allay some of this natural anxiety by communicating clear expectations and by having suitable procedures, rules, and reasonable consequences. Such features add structure to the classroom by making it a more predictable place; students may accept this structure because it gives them more personal control over the consequences that are likely to occur.

Finally, it is easier to teach appropriate behavior before inappropriate behavior becomes established. Once students develop a pattern of inappropriate behavior, the teacher's task of obtaining desirable behaviors is complicated by the need to extinguish the undesirable ones.

The choice of activities during the first several days of the school year should be determined largely by two complementary perspectives: the teacher's need to implement the planned system for classroom management and the students' need for information about the classroom setting and school-related tasks. Our observations of effective classroom managers suggest the following principles as the basis for beginning-of-year activities.

1. *Teachers should set aside some time during the first day or first class meeting for a discussion of rules.* Because rules are usually general statements of expected behavior, their use as cues for appropriate behavior depends on the students' ability to identify relevant behaviors. During the first several weeks, this can be accomplished if the teacher points out instances of desirable behaviors and the rules to which they refer. Another way to help students learn rules is to review them at the end of a period or a day, noting ways in which the class has behaved appropriately.

2. *Teachers should teach classroom procedures as systematically as any other learning objective.* The teacher should clearly explain and demonstrate what behaviors are desired, and identify the context or setting in which they are expected to occur. In the elementary grades in particular, children should be given the opportunity to practice the behaviors. Even junior high students profit from practicing complex procedures or those that are safety related. The teacher must carefully watch practice trials or initial attempts to follow a procedure in order to provide corrective feedback and to see the procedure followed through to completion.

3. *Teachers should teach procedures as they are needed by students to help them negotiate the classroom setting.* For example, procedures for using the bathroom, drinking fountain, and desks, and procedures for lining up, passing in the hallways, and doing seatwork generally should be taught on the first day because each will be used during that time. However, procedures for small groups need not be taught until that format is actually used. In most elementary classrooms, teachers need several weeks to teach procedures as they introduce content. At early elementary grade levels an even longer time may be needed before classes finally "settle in" to routines.

4. Teachers should involve children in easy tasks and promote a high rate of success for the first few days of school. Early success promotes a positive outlook for the year and makes task engagement easy, whereas task avoidance is promoted by early failure. Furthermore, if early tasks are too involved or difficult, the teacher's attention is likely to be diverted by the problems of individual students, at the very time when the teacher's skills are needed to monitor the whole class.

5. Teachers should use only those activities and formats with a whole-group focus or which require simple procedures, at least for the first several days. A whole-group focus means presenting information or giving directions to everyone in the class at the same time, and providing the same assignments for everyone. Behavior is easier to monitor in whole-group settings, and fewer procedures are needed than with small-group or individualized instruction. After students have learned appropriate behavior in the simpler settings and have demonstrated their capability for following general classroom rules, then they will be ready for more complex procedures. Also, by then the teacher will have a better idea about which students will need close supervision when attempting new formats.

6. Teachers should include in their lesson plans provisions for teaching rules and procedures where appropriate. Extra time should be allotted to teach new activities and their attendant procedures. For example, in addition to directions for a particular activity and the time needed to accomplish it, students about to engage for the first time in a seatwork assignment need to know what paper or other material should be used, the correct form for heading or placing a name on the material, what to do with completed work, and what to do afterward.

7. Teachers should not assume students know how to perform a procedure after one trial. Complex procedures particuarly should be reviewed several times, perhaps using a question and answer or recitation format to verify student understanding. Once students can read, complex procedures can be written out and displayed. For example, procedures for using a learning center, laboratory equipment, or other materials will be more likely followed if they are posted in the area. Likewise, grading procedures, particularly when they are complicated, might be reproduced on a ditto handout and given to students or even sent home.

Maintaining an Effective Management System Throughout the Year

Up to this point we have emphasized the need for extensive planning to achieve good management results, and described many of the important areas to be considered. We now turn our attention to a series of teaching skills and instructional features that are evident in the teaching styles of good managers.

Monitoring student behavior. One cornerstone of an effective management system is the careful monitoring of student behavior. Monitoring is necessary because it can detect minor student problems before they become major ones. Monitoring means both watching or attending to student behavior in the classroom and keeping track of student progress on assignments and in other learning activities. Particularly at the beginning of the year, teachers should focus on initial student tasks such as following procedures and completing assignments. Carefully monitoring students' adherence to classroom procedures and rules can help detect inappropriate behavior and clarify misunderstandings if they exist, thus allowing teachers to correct misbehavior before it spreads and becomes a problem.

The level of student success in assigned tasks should be monitored because failure to perform work can lead students to avoid involvement or to escape through active disruption. If high failure rates occur, teachers should reconsider their instructional approaches, improve explanations, reteach the material with another approach, or give assignments or tasks more appropriate to the students' level of mastery. Students' success or failure can be checked by a careful review of their written work and assignments, both during seatwork and after assignments have been completed and turned in. Even if self-checking or exchanging papers with other students is used, the teacher should examine a portion of students' work daily or at regular times during the week. Teachers can also look for confusion, copying, completing work very early, or unusually slow progress. Some of this behavior can occur in any class, but consistent evidence suggests that reteaching or additional help may be in order. Teachers can also look for attending behaviors, such as eyes to the front of the room, pencils or pens on the desk, and appropriate materials ready for use.

Many teachers need to practice their monitoring. For example, during whole-class instruction, some teachers maintain eye contact with only a small number of children. When teachers work with small groups and the remaining children in the class are at seatwork, poor monitors seldom look up from their group to scan the class until some loud noise or disruption occurs. Sometimes teachers locate the small group where they are not in a position to observe the whole class. In such circumstances, the teacher cannot prevent inappropriate behavior from occurring, and instead will only be able to react to it once it becomes disruptive. Thus, teachers need to make a conscious effort to scan the room frequently during whole-class instruction, and speak to all students in the class rather than focusing on those nearest or in a direct line of sight. Teachers should move around the room during seatwork and check on student progress, rather than becoming engrossed with one or a few students. Finally, teachers must be careful to keep lines of sight open and avoid having students mill about them at their desks or in the small-group area.

There are a number of strategies for monitoring student progress in assignments. Frequently when a class or group is given a seatwork assignment, teachers will immediately begin working with another group or with individual students; unfortunately, some students may not begin their work promptly or may not understand what they are to do. Therefore, teachers should be especially careful to watch students for a few minutes at the beginning of seatwork. If problems are noted, then the teacher can deal with them immediately. In addition, student work needs to be checked regularly and good recordkeeping practiced. The teacher can then easily identify students whose level of work is lacking or who are not completing or turning in assignments. Again, it is much easier to deal with and to resolve these problems when they first occur than it is to try to correct them after they have become an established pattern of behavior. When longer term assignments or projects are being used, monitoring should include check points at frequent intervals. Finally, teachers may occasionally wish to focus on a particular behavior that is becoming disruptive. Noting the time of day or activity in which it occurs and observing closely for causes will help identify the correct intervention.

Managing inappropriate behavior. Inappropriate behavior thrives when the teacher ignores it. If inappropriate behavior continues unchecked, more students violate rules or fail to follow correct procedures, and consequently, become confused about what correct behavior is. Student avoidance of work also has the potential for escalation, because students who fail to complete assignments initially may not learn what is needed to perform adequately in subsequent lessons. Furthermore, widespread task avoidance may lead to a counter-productive norm. In such a circumstance, students may begin to resist seatwork or homework and support one another's avoidance when the teacher attempts to engage them in work. Clearly, it is better to stop most inappropriate behavior quickly. Early intervention establishes the credibility of rules and procedures, and demonstrates that the teacher is going to use the system.

Teachers in our studies usually used direct, simple means of dealing with failure to follow procedures or rules. These teacher actions typically were straightforward requests or signals for appropriate behavior. Generally speaking, good managers avoid over-reaction and emotionality; rather, the student is regarded as simply not having learned the correct procedures. The perspective that seems most useful is helping the student learn how to behave appropriately. Effective managers often use these common and simple procedures:

1. Ask the student to stop the inappropriate behavior. The teacher maintains contact with the child until the appropriate behavior is correctly performed.

2. Make eye-contact with the student until appropriate behavior returns. This is suitable when the teacher is certain the student knows what the correct procedure is.

3. Restate or remind the student of the correct rule or procedure.

4. Ask the student to identify the correct procedure. Give feedback if the student does not understand it.

5. Impose the consequence or penalty of the rule or procedure violation. Usually, the consequence for violating a procedure is simply to perform the procedure until it is correctly done. When the student understands the procedure and is not complying in order to receive attention or for other inappropriate reasons, the teacher can use a mild penalty, such as withholding a privilege.

6. Change the activity. Frequently, off-task behavior occurs when students are engaged too long in repetitive, boring tasks or in aimless recitations. Injecting variety in seatwork, refocusing discussion, or changing the activity to one requiring another type of student response, is appropriate when off-task behavior spreads widely throughout a class.

Serious disruption should usually be handled either by removing the student from the setting, such as to the hallway or to a quiet area away from other students, or by invoking some consequences or penalty for the disruptive behavior. When the school has a procedure for coping with such behavior, the teacher should use it. Following up such incidents by conferring with the student, calling parents, or meeting with school counselors or other personnel may be helpful in determining what led to the behavior and how to prevent it in the future.

Although these procedures are generally simple to apply and do not greatly disturb classroom routines, there may be times when the teacher will find it inappropriate to intervene—for instance, when (a) the problem is momentary, (b) the problem is not serious or dangerous, (c) drawing attention to the behavior would seriously impede the activity in progress, (d) the student is normally well-behaved, and (e) other students are not involved. In these circumstances there is relatively little likelihood that the situation will escalate into widespread misbehavior, interfere with learning, or cause students to become confused about what is correct and incorrect behavior. When such behavior is deliberately ignored, the teacher should make a mental note to monitor the situation closely.

Developing student accountability. Effective classroom managers teach students to be responsible for participating in class and completing their assigned work. There are six aspects of developing student accountability.

1. *Clarity of work assignments.* The teacher must have a specific set of expectations for student performance, covering such details as the form of student work, expectations regarding neatness, completeness, due dates, and procedures for make-up work. The specific requirements in these areas may vary greatly from teacher to teacher, according to the subject content and age level of the students, and the personal preferences of the teacher. The teacher should try to decide what is reasonable, given the teaching context, and what will aid students in the development of good work habits. Then these requirements should be communicated to the students. Having such procedures does not assure the teacher that all students will follow them, but at least it will provide the teacher with a basis for giving students relevant feedback. It will also let the students know how to attend to these important details.

2. *Communicating assignments.* Assignments should be clear, so that every student understands what to do. This can be accomplished in several ways. Establishing a routine for posting assignments in a particular place or having students copy assignments onto their worksheet or paper assures that everyone will at least be able to find out what the assignment is, even when the teacher is not available to point it out to them. Grading requirements should be spelled out to students, so that they know exactly what the teacher considers important in assessing achievement. Long-term assignments require great care in setting up with younger children. It is a good idea to divide projects into steps and provide students with a description of what is to be done at each step.

3. *Monitoring student work.* Once assignments are made and students begin work, it is again essential that the teacher be aware of student progress. This can be accomplished by circulating throughout the classroom and systematically checking each student's work. The teacher should scan the class for a minute or two at the beginning of a seatwork activity to make sure that everyone has begun. If getting started on seatwork is a problem, the teacher may elect to begin the first part of the assignment with the class as a whole, allowing a few minutes for everyone to get out the proper materials, get headings and the assignment properly copied, and work a problem or do a sample exercise. Once the teacher is sure everyone understands the task and has begun work, then he or she may circulate around the room and assist individual students. During recitation or discussion activities, as well as small-group work, the teacher should also monitor student involvement. The teacher may wish to use some systematic process for obtaining student responses, such as calling names from a class

roster or using a pattern, rather than relying on volunteers to answer questions. A sustained pattern of using only volunteers allows many students in a class to avoid involvement.

4. *Checking work*. Once assignments have been completed, the teacher needs a system for checking work. Assignments that have specific answers may be checked by students. This provides quick feedback to each student, although the teacher should be sure to establish procedures for checking. A procedure is also needed for students to turn in their papers. Certain assignments may be put in a basket at the front of the room, and a special area may be designated for collecting and returning assignments of absent students.

5. *Giving feedback to students*. It is through practice and feedback that most instruction begins to pay off in learning. When students receive information about their performance, they obtain the basis for improvement. Regular routines for checking work and returning it to students are useful. It is also helpful if teachers set aside some time after assignments have been returned for the students to review their papers and make corrections. Of course, it would be ideal for teachers to catch student errors while the student was first working on the assignment. Then corrective feedback could be given before a student learned an incorrect response. When this cannot be done, however, the teacher must rely on students making corrections after receiving materials back. The feedback older students receive is usually tied in with a grading system; therefore, the teacher needs an overall basis for grading consistent with the instructional goals. One technique is to have students keep a record of their work in each grading period. The teacher may provide students with a ditto sheet that has space for recording assignments, test grades, project grades, or any other course requirement. Students then maintain this record throughout the grading period. Such a procedure is quite effective in helping students understand the relationship between their performance and grades. It also can be a useful tool for communicating with parents about their child's performance.

6. *Clarity in instructions*. Most effective managers give clear and specific instructions, which is an instructional and a managerial asset. Clear instruction of academic content helps students succeed and learn; unclear instruction can produce failure, frustration, and task avoidance. Clarity is aided by a number of factors. First, the teacher must have a very good idea of what is to be taught and how. Therefore, planning is essential. Second, the teacher must communicate information so that students understand it. Thus, the teacher's awareness of student comprehension is critical. Third, the precision and clarity of the teacher's oral expression are important. Sloppy speech habits lead to vagueness and confusion.

Following are suggestions to help teachers provide clear instruction.

a. Anticipate problems and difficulties students are likely to have when new concepts and skills are introduced. When teaching a new age level, grade level, or a new subject, the teacher is least likely to anticipate student problems. Before instruction begins, the teacher should actually perform assignments or tasks that are to be given to students, identify any terms that may be new to students, read curriculum guides and instructors manuals carefully, and ask colleagues about common student problems and suggestions for dealing with them. During instruction, the teacher should avoid digressions, interruptions, and irrelevancies. Except for necessary review and reteaching, teachers should stick with the logical sequence in the lesson plans, making each point in the relationships between parts of the lesson very clear.

b. Check student comprehension periodically as lessons progress. One way to check comprehension is to ask students to repeat directions or to summarize the main idea of some part of a lesson. Modeling correct behavior is highly desirable when teaching a skill, rather than simply focusing on correcting wrong responses. When learning a skill, students must be given a chance to practice it; the teacher needs to look for correct and incorrect performance. When teaching a concept or principle, questions should be planned to test comprehension at various points during the presentation, rather than only at the end.

c. Practice good oral communication skills by using clear, precise language. By writing words and their definitions on the board whenever a new word is used, teachers will help students understand the vocabulary. Teachers whose presentations tend to wander, or who sometimes skip important parts of a lesson, may find it helpful to put a short outline of the topic on the chalkboard.

Conclusion

We have made a number of recommendations for developing effective classroom management procedures. These recommendations considered three major phases: planning before the year begins, beginning the year, and maintaining good classroom management. A major assumption underlying each of our suggestions is the teacher's responsibility for organizing the classroom environment to bring about student involvement in learning tasks and to minimize disruptive and inappropriate behaviors. Within that perspective, our recommendation can accommodate a variety of contexts and instructional approaches.

References

Anderson, L.; Evertson, C.; and Emmer E. "Dimensions in Classroom Management Derived From Recent Research." *Journal of Curriculum Studies* 12 (1980): 343-356.

Bloom, B. *Human Characteristics and School Learning.* New York: McGraw-Hill, 1976.

Brophy, J. "Teacher Behavior and Its Effects." *Journal of Educational Psychology* 71 (1979): 733-750.

Dunkin, M., and Biddle, B. *The Study of Teaching.* New York: Holt, Rinehart and Winston, 1974.

Emmer, E.; Evertson, C.; and Anderson, L. "Effective Classroom Management at the Beginning of the School Year." *Elementary School Journal* 80 (1980): 219-231.

Evertson, C., and Emmer, E. "Effective Management at the Beginning of the School Year in Junior High Classes." *Journal of Educational Psychology* (in press).

Evertson, C.; Sanford, J.; and Emmer, E. "Effects of Class Heterogeneity in Junior High School." *American Educational Research Journal* 18 (1981): 219-232.

Good, T. L. "Teacher Effectiveness in the Elementary School: What We Know About It Now." *Journal of Teacher Education* 30 (1979): 32-64.

Jackson, P. *Life in Classrooms.* New York: Holt, Rinehart and Winston, 1968.

Lortie, D. *Schoolteacher: A Sociological Study.* Chicago: The University of Chicago Press, 1975.

Medley, D. *Teacher Competence and Teacher Effectiveness: A Review of Process-Product Research.* Washington, D.C.: American Association of Colleges for Teacher Education, 1977.

Sanford, J., and Evertson, C. "Classroom Management in a Low SES Junior High: Three Case Studies." *Journal of Teacher Education* 32 (1981): 34-38.

Conducting large-scale studies of classroom teaching requires the work of many people. The authors wish to acknowledge and thank the following people whose contributions were invaluable: Linda M. Anderson, former associate director of the project who helped conceptualize and design our first study of classroom management, and Barbara S. Clements, Julie P. Sanford, Murray E. Worsham, Ellen L. Williams, and Jeanne Martin.

2

Supplemental Group Management Techniques

Jere Brophy

THE key to effective classroom management is indeed prevention: effective classroom managers are distinguished by their success in preventing problems from arising in the first place, rather than by special skills for dealing with problems once they occur. It is clear that their success is not achieved through a few isolated techniques or gimmicks. It is instead the result of a systematic approach to classroom management, which starts with advanced preparation and planning before the school year begins, is implemented initially through systematic communication of expectations and establishment of procedures and routines at the beginning of the year, and is maintained through the year, not only by consistency in following up on stated expectations, but by presenting students with a continuous stream of well-chosen and well-prepared academic activities that focus their attention during group lessons and engage their concentrated efforts during independent work times.

Such a thorough and integrated approach to classroom management, if implemented continuously and linked with similarly thorough and effective instruction, will enable teachers to prevent most problems from occurring in the first place and to handle those that do occur with brief, nondisruptive techniques. This approach appears to be both necessary (less intensive or systematic efforts are unlikely to succeed) and sufficient (the teacher establishes the classroom as an effective learning environment without requiring more intensive or cumbersome techniques such as token economies). Yet, some students with intensive personal or behavioral

This chapter is an excerpt from a paper presented before a conference sponsored by the National Institute of Education at Airlie House, Warrenton, Virginia, February 1982. Preparation of this chapter was supported by the Institute for Research on Teaching, College of Education, Michigan State University. The Institute is funded primarily by the Teaching Division of the National Institute of Education. The opinions expressed in this publication do not necessarily reflect the position, policy, or endorsement of NIE.

problems will require individualized treatment in addition to (not instead of) group management techniques. Many teachers will want to pursue broader student socialization goals beyond establishing the classroom as an effective learning environment—developing good group dynamics, promoting individuals' mental health and personal adjustment, and so forth. Special techniques can and should be used for these purposes, although it should be recognized that they are supplements to and not substitutes for basic techniques such as those described in Chapter 1 by Evertson and Emmer and elsewhere by Kounin (1970).

Additional Group Management Techniques

Group Relationships

Recent research has produced a great deal of information useful to teachers concerned about establishing good interpersonal relationships and group dynamics in their classrooms, including information about how to overcome the social barriers that are often associated with differences in sex, race, social class, or achievement level. This research makes it clear that merely bringing antagonistic or voluntarily segregated groups together for frequent contact will not by itself promote prosocial, integrated activities. In fact, it may even increase the level of group conflict. Prosocial outcomes can be expected, however, when students from different groups are involved in cooperative activities—especially interdependent activities that require the active participation of all group members to ensure successful accomplishment of the group mission (Aronson and others, 1978; Johnson and Johnson, 1975; Sharan, 1980; Slavin, 1980).

An example is the Jigsaw approach (Aronson and others, 1978), in which group activities are arranged so that each member of the group possesses at least one key item of unique information that is essential to the group's success. This requires the brighter and more assertive students who might ordinarily dominate group interaction to the exclusion of their peers (Webb, 1980) to encourage the active participation of everyone, and to value everyone's contribution. It also encourages the slower and more reticent students, who might otherwise contribute little or nothing, to participate actively in group activities and consider themselves as true group members and important contributors.

The Teams-Games-Tournaments (TGT) approach accomplishes similar goals in a different way (Slavin, 1980). Here, students are divided into teams (in which members vary in sex, race, achievement level, and so on) who compete for prizes awarded for academic excellence. In addition to working together as a team on whatever cooperative activities may be included in the program, team members contribute to their team's point totals through their performance on seatwork and other independent activities. Each team member contributes roughly equally to the team's relative success, because points are awarded according to a handicapping system in which performance standards are based on each individual's previous levels of success. Thus, low achievers who succeed in meeting the performance standards assigned to them contribute as much to their team's total score as high achievers who succeed in meeting the performance standards assigned to them. This approach has been shown to improve the quality and quantity of contact among team members inside and outside of the classroom, and it sometimes leads to improved achievement in addition to improved interpersonal relationships (Slavin, 1980).

Other approaches in which group members cooperate to pursue common goals have been successful in promoting good group dynamics (see Stanford, 1977, regarding the formation and development of classroom groups), and approaches that allow individuals to display unique knowledge or skills have been successful in enhancing the social status or peer acceptance of the individuals involved. In general, successful techniques have in common the fact that they do not merely bring together individuals who do not often interact, but bring them together in ways that require them to cooperate prosocially or allow them to see positive attributes in one another that they might not have become aware of otherwise. In addition to these group-based approaches, there are a variety of social skills training approaches that teachers can use to coach socially isolated or rejected students in such skills as initiating interactions with their peers, reinforcing prosocial contact, and the like (Cartledge and Milburn, 1978).

Behavior Modification Techniques

Techniques of behavior analysis and behavior modification are often recommended to teachers based on social learning theory: reward desirable behavior and extinguish (by ignoring) undesirable behavior, or if necessary, punish undesirable behavior (O'Leary and O'Leary, 1977; Krumboltz and Krumboltz, 1972). Early applications were mostly limited to the shaping of the behaviors (such as staying in the seat or remaining quiet) of individual students through material reinforcement. Since then, systems have been developed for use with the class as a whole (Thompson and others, 1974) and the emphasis has shifted from inhibiting misconduct to rewarding good academic performance (Kazdin, 1977) and from controlling students externally to teaching them to control themselves

(Meichenbaum, 1977; McLaughlin, 1976). The techniques have pro-liferated. Procedures for increasing desired behavior include praise and approval, modeling, token reinforcement programs, programmed instruction, self-specification of contingencies, self-reinforcement, establishment of clear rules and directions, and shaping. Procedures for decreasing un-desired behavior include extinction, reinforcing incompatible behaviors, self-reprimands, time out from reinforcement, relaxation (for fears and anxiety), response cost (punishment by removal of reinforcement), medication, self-instruction, and self-evaluation. The breadth of this list indicates the practical orientation of contemporary behavior modifiers, as well as the degree to which they have embraced techniques that originated elsewhere and that have little or nothing to do with social learning theory or reinforcement.

Most of the early, reinforcement-oriented behavior modification ap-proaches proved impractical for most teachers. For example, the financial and time costs involved in implementing token economy systems make these approaches unacceptable to most teachers. Token economies have been popular with special education teachers working in resource rooms where individualized learning programs and a low student-teacher ratio make them more feasible (Safer and Allen, 1976).

Approaches based on social rather than material reinforcement are less cumbersome, but they have problems of their own. For one thing, a single teacher working with a class of 30 students will not even be able to keep track of, let alone systematically reinforce, all of the desirable be-haviors of each individual student (Emery and Marholin, 1977). Secondly, praise and other forms of social reinforcement by teachers do not have powerful effects on most students, at least after the first grade or two in school. Thirdly, the "praise and ignore" formula has inherent drawbacks that limit its effectiveness in classroom situations. *Praising the desirable behavior of classmates is a less efficient method of shaping the behavior of the target student than more direct instruction or cuing would be.* Further-more, ignoring undesirable behavior will have the effect of extinguishing it only if the behavior is being reinforced by teacher attention. This is probably true of only a small minority of the undesirable behavior that students display, and even where it is true, ignoring the problem may lead to escalation in intensity or spread to other students, as Kounin (1970) has shown. Thus, the principles of extinction through ignoring and shap-ing behavior through vicarious reinforcement delivered to the peers of the target student cannot be applied often in the ordinary classroom. They certainly cannot be used as the basis for a systematic approach to class-room management.

Reinforcement can be used efficiently to shape behavior when it is applied directly to the target student and delivered as a consequence of the performance of desired behavior (at least to some degree; it has become clear that the reinforcers under the control of most teachers are numerous but weak, so that certain behaviors by certain students cannot literally be controlled by teacher-administered reinforcement). Although this can bring about desired behavior and even academic performance, it does so through processes of extrinsic reinforcement, which may reduce the degree to which students find working on or completing school tasks to be intrinsically rewarding (Lepper and Greene, 1978). The degree to which this is likely to occur depends on the degree to which students are led to believe they are performing solely to obtain the extrinsic rewards, and not because the performance is inherently satisfying or involves the acquisition or exercise of valued skills.

Thus, the motivational effect of controlling students' behavior through reinforcement will be determined by the meanings the students are led to attribute to the reinforcement process.

The guidelines in Figure 1, drawn from the work of several attribution theorists, can help direct teachers' use of praise in ways that would not only shape students' behavior, but encourage their development of associated intrinsic motivation. The same guidelines apply to the use of any reinforcer, not just praise. The principles summarized in Figure 1 stress teaching students how to think about their behavior rather than merely reinforcing it. They also stress the development of self-monitoring and self-control. They are represenatative of the general changes that have been introduced into applications of behavior modification to classrooms.

For example, teachers desiring to shape student behavior through reinforcement are now being advised not merely to reinforce contingently, but to draw up a formal contract with the student in advance, specifying precisely the performance standards that must be attained to earn the promised rewards. This "contingency contracting" approach can be used to specify improvements in both conduct and academic performance. The technique allows teachers to individualize arrangements with separate students. It also places more emphasis on student self-control, self-management, and self-instruction, and less on one-to-one relationships between specific behaviors and specific rewards. Contracts can be helpful in dealing with students who are poorly motivated, easily distracted, or resistant to school work or to the teacher.

Experience with some of the elements involved in contingency contracting, such as goal setting and self-monitoring of behavior, led to the realization that these elements can have important positive effects of their own, independent of reinforcement. For example, inducing students to

Figure 1. Guidelines for Effective Praise

Effective Praise:

1. is delivered contingently
2. specifies the particulars of the accomplishment
3. shows spontaneity, variety, and other signs of credibility; suggests clear attention to the student's accomplishment
4. rewards attainment of specified performance criteria (which can include effort criteria)
5. provides information to students about their competence or the value of their accomplishments
6. orients students toward better appreciation of their own task-related behavior and thinking about problem solving
7. uses student's own prior accomplishments as the context for describing present accomplishments
8. is given in recognition of noteworthy effort or success at difficult (for this student) tasks.
9. attributes success to effort and ability, implying that similar successes can be expected in the future
10. fosters endogenous attributions (students believe they expend effort on task because they enjoy it and/or want to develop task-relevant skills)
11. focuses students' attention on their own task-relevant behavior
12. fosters appreciation of, and desirable attributions about, task-relevant behavior after the process is completed

Ineffective Praise:

1. is delivered randomly or unsystematically
2. is restricted to global positive reactions
3. shows a bland uniformity that suggests a conditioned response made with minimal attention
4. rewards mere participation, without consideration of performance processes or outcomes
5. provides no information at all or gives students information about their status
6. orients students toward comparing themselves with others and thinking about competing
7. uses the accomplishments of peers as the context for describing students' present accomplishments
8. is given without regard to the effort expended or the meaning of the accomplishment (for *this* student)
9. attributes success to ability alone or to external factors such as luck or (easy) task difficulty
10. fosters exogenous attributions (students believe they expend effort on the task for external reasons—to please the teacher, win a competition or reward, etc.)
11. focuses students' attention on the teacher as an external authority figure who is manipulating them
12. intrudes into the ongoing process, distracting attention from task-relevant behavior

From Jere E. Brophy, "Teacher Praise: A Functional Analysis." *Review of Educational Research* (Spring 1981): 5-32. Washington, D.C.: American Educational Research Association, 1981.

set goals for themselves can lead to performance increases, especially if those goals are specific and difficult rather than vague or too easy (Rosswork, 1977). Apparently, engaging in the process of setting goals not only provides students with specific objectives to pursue, but leads them to concentrate their efforts and monitor their performance more closely. The process does not work always or automatically, however. Sagotsky and others (1978) found that exposure to goal-setting procedures had no significant effect on students' study behavior or academic achievement, largely because many of the students did not follow through by actually using the goal-setting procedures they had been shown.

That same study did show the effectiveness of self-monitoring procedures, however. Students taught to monitor and maintain daily records of their own study behavior showed significant increases in both study behavior and tested achievement (Sagotsky and others, 1978). This was but one of many studies illustrating the effectiveness of procedures designed to help students monitor their own classroom behavior more closely and control it more effectively (Glynn and others, 1973; McLaughlin, 1976; O'Leary and Dubey, 1979; Rosenbaum and Drabman, 1979).

These procedures, based on developing self-control in students, have two potential advantages over earlier procedures that depended on external control by the teacher (to the extent that they are implemented successfully). First, as noted previously, reinforcement-oriented approaches to classroom management that depend on the teacher as the dispenser of reinforcement are impractical in the typical classroom, where a single teacher must deal with 30 students. Even the most skillful and determined teacher cannot continuously monitor all of the students and reinforce all of them appropriately. When responsibility for monitoring (and perhaps reinforcing) performance is shifted from the teacher to the students, this bottleneck is removed. Second, to the extent that teachers are successful in using behavior modification methods to shape student behavior, the effects depend on the presence and activity of the teacher and thus do not generalize to other settings nor persist beyond the term or school year. Again, to the extent that students can learn to monitor and control their own behavior in school, they may also be able to generalize and apply these self-control skills in other classrooms or even in nonschool settings.

Self-control skills are typically taught to students using a variety of recently developed procedures that Meichenbaum (1977) has called "cognitive behavior modification." One such technique combines modeling with verbalized self-instructions. Rather than just tell students what to do, the model (teacher) demonstrates the process. The demonstration includes not only the physical motions involved, but verbalization of the thoughts and other self-talk (self-instructions, self-monitoring, self-reinforcement) that would accompany the physical motions involved in doing the task.

For example, Meichenbaum and Goodman (1971) used the technique with cognitively impulsive students who made many errors on a matching-to-sample task because they would respond too quickly, settling on the first response alternative that looked correct rather than taking time to examine all of the response alternatives before selecting the best one. Earlier studies had shown that simply telling these students to take their time, or even requiring them to inhibit their response for a specified delay period, did not improve their performance because the students did not use this time to examine the available alternatives. They simply waited until the time period was up. However, the technique of modeling with verbalized self-instructions stressed the importance of carefully observing each alternative. As the models "thought out loud" while demonstrating the task, they made a point of resisting the temptation to settle on an alternative that looked correct before examining all of the rest, reminded themselves that one can be fooled by small differences in detail that are not noticed at first, and so on. This approach was successful in improving performance on the task, because the students learned to carefully compare each alternative with the model before selecting their response. Rather than merely imposing a delay on their speed of response, the treatment presented them with a strategy for responding to the task successfully, and presented this strategy in a form that the students could easily understand and apply themselves.

Modeling combined with verbalized self-instructions (as well as various related role play approaches) can be helpful with a great variety of student problems. Meichenbaum (1977) describes five stages to this approach:

(1) an adult models a task while speaking aloud (cognitive modeling);

(2) the child performs the task under the model's instruction (overt, external guidance);

(3) the child performs the task while verbalizing self-instructions aloud (overt self-guidance);

(4) the child whispers self-instructions while doing the task (faded overt self-guidance);

(5) the child performs the task under self guidance via private speech (covert self-instruction).

Variations of this approach have been used not only to teach cognitively impulsive children to approach tasks more effectively, but also to help social isolates learn to initiate activities with their peers, to teach students to be more creative in problem solving, to help aggressive students learn to control their anger and respond more effectively to frustration, and to help frustrated and defeated students learn to cope with failure and respond to mistakes with problem-solving efforts rather than withdrawal or resignation.

Recent applications include the "turtle" technique of Robin and others (1976), in which teachers teach impulsive and aggressive students to assume the "turtle" position when upset. The students learn to place their heads on their desks, close their eyes, and clench their fists. This gives them an immediate response to use in anger-provoking situations, and buys time that enables them to delay inappropriate behavior and think about constructive solutions to the problem. The "turtle" position is actually not essential; the key is training children to delay impulsive responding while they gradually relax and think about constructive alternatives. However, it is a gimmick that many younger students find enjoyable, and may also serve as a sort of crutch to certain children who might otherwise not be able to delay successfully.

Similarly, the "Think Aloud" program of Camp and Bash (1981) is designed to teach children to use their cognitive skills to guide their social behavior and to learn to cope with social problems. It is especially useful with students in the early grades, especially those prone to paranoid interpretations of peers' behavior or aggressive acting out as a response to frustration. In general, although generalization of skills taught through cognitive interventions has not yet been demonstrated convincingly (Pressley, 1979), approaches featuring modeling, verbalized self-instructions, and other aspects of self-monitoring and self-control training appear to be very promising for use in classrooms, both as instructional techniques for students and as remediation techniques for students with emotional or behavioral problems (McLaughlin, 1976; O'Leary and Dubey, 1979; Rosenbaum and Drabman, 1979).

Individual Counseling and Therapy

In addition to behavior modification techniques, a variety of techques developed by counselors and psychotherapists have been recommended for use by teachers with students who have chronic personal or behavioral problems. Early on, many of these approaches stressed psychoanalytic or other "depth" interpretation of behavior and treatment through methods such as free association or acting out of impulses against substitute objects to achieve catharsis or gratification. Many of these early theories have proven unnecessary or incorrect, and the early treatment methods have proven ineffective or unfeasible for consistent use by most teachers.

More recently, however, therapy-based suggestions to teachers have shifted concern from unconscious motivations to overt behaviors, from long-term general treatment toward briefer crisis intervention, and from viewing disturbed students as "sick" toward viewing them as needing information or insight that will allow them to understand themselves better and achieve better control over their emotions and behavior. As a result, these therapy-based notions have become more compatible with one another and with the cognitive behavior modification approaches described above. Suggestions from different sources are mostly complementary rather than contradictory; taken together they provide the basis for systematic approaches to counseling problem students.

Dreikurs (1968) sees disturbed students as reacting to their own feelings of discouragement or inferiority by developing defense mechanisms designed to protect self-esteem. He believes that students who do not work out satisfactory personal and group adjustments at school will display symptoms related to seeking after one of the following goals (listed in increasing order of disturbance): attention, power, revenge, or display of inferiority. He then suggests how teachers can determine the purpose of student symptoms by analyzing the goals the students seem to be pursuing and the effects the students' behavior seems to be having on the teacher. He also suggests ways teachers can use this information to help students eliminate their need to continue such behavior.

Morse (1971) describes the "life space interview," in which teachers work together with students until each understands troublesome incidents and their meanings to the student, and until ways to prevent repetition of the problem are identified. During these interviews, the teacher lets the students get things off their chests and makes an effort to appreciate their perceptions and beliefs. At the same time, the teacher forces the students to confront unpleasant realities, helps them develop new or deeper insights, and, following emotional catharsis and problem analysis, seeks to find mutually agreed upon solutions.

Good and Brophy (1978, 1980) present similar advice about maintaining a neutral but solution-oriented stance in dealing with student conflict, conducting investigations in ways that are likely to obtain the desired information and avoid escalating the conflict, negotiating agreements about proposed solutions, obtaining commitment, and promoting growth through modeling and communication of positive expectations.

Gordon (1974) discusses the need to analyze the degree to which parties to a conflict "own" the problem. The problem is owned by the teacher but not the student if only the teacher's needs are being frustrated (as when a student persistently disrupts the class by socializing with friends). Conversely, the student owns the problem when the student's needs are being frustrated (such as when a student is rejected by the peer group through no fault of the teacher). Finally, teachers and students share problems in situations where each is frustrating the needs of the other.

Gordon believes that student-owned problems call for a generally sympathetic and helpful stance, and in particular, an attempt to understand and clarify the student's problem through "active listening." During active listening, the teacher not only listens carefully to the student's message, tries to understand it from the student's point of view, and reflects it back accurately to the student, but also listens for the personal feelings and reactions of the student to the events being described, and reflects understanding of these to the student, as well. When the teacher owns the problem, it is necessary for the teacher to communicate the problem to the student, using "I" messages that state explicitly the linkages between the student's problem behavior, the problem that the behavior causes the teacher (how it frustrates the teacher's needs), and the effects of these events on the teacher's feelings (discouragement, frustration). The idea here is to minimize blame and ventilation of anger, and to get the student not only to recognize the problem behavior itself but to see its effects on the teacher.

Active listening and "I" messages will help teachers and students to achieve shared rational views of problems, and help them to assume a cooperative, problem-solving attitude. To the extent that conflicts are involved, Gordon recommends a "no lose" method of finding the solution that will work best for all concerned. The six steps in the process are: define the problem; generate possible solutions; evaluate those solutions; decide which is best; determine how to implement this decision; and assess how well the solution is working later (with negotiation of the new agreement if the solution is not working satisfactorily to all concerned)..

Glasser (1969, 1977) has suggested applications of what he calls "reality therapy" to teachers, providing guidelines for both general classroom management and problem solving with individual students. The title of his book, *Schools Without Failure* (Glasser, 1969) illustrates his interest in a facilitative atmosphere in the school at large, and not just in individual teacher-student relationships. In that book he advocated that classroom meetings be used for teachers and students to jointly establish classroom rules, adjust these rules, develop new ones when needed, and deal with problems. This part of his approach is not as well accepted as his later suggestions, because many teachers oppose student self-government on principle, and others find it overly cumbersome and time consuming. Also, it can involve exposure of vulnerable individuals to public scrutiny and pressure, violation of confidences, and other ethical problems.

More recently, Glasser (1977) has advanced what he calls his "ten steps to good discipline," which he describes as a constructive and non-punitive but no-nonsense approach. It is predicated on the beliefs that: students are and will be held responsible for their in-school behavior; rules are reasonable and fairly administered; and teachers maintain a positive problem-solving stance in dealing with students.

Glasser's ten-step approach is intended for use with students who have not responded to generally effective classroom management. Each consecutive step escalates the seriousness of the problem, and thus should not be implemented lightly. The ten steps are:

1. Select a student for concentrated attention and list typical reactions to the student's disruptive behavior.

2. Analyze the list to see what techniques do and do not work and resolve not to repeat the ones that do not work.

3. Improve personal relationships with the student by providing extra encouragement, asking the student to perform special errands, showing concern, implying that things will improve, and so forth.

4. Focus the student's attention on the disruptive behavior by requiring the student to describe what he or she has been doing. Continue until the student describes the behavior accurately, and then request that he or she stop it.

5. Call a short conference. Again have the student describe the behavior and state whether or not it is against the rules or recognized expectations. Then ask the student what he or she should be doing instead.

6. Repeat step five, but this time add that a plan will be needed to solve the problem. The plan will be more than a simple agreement to stop misbehaving, because this has not been honored in the past. The negotiated plan must include the student's commitment to positive actions designed to eliminate the problem.

7. Isolate the student or use time-out procedures. During these periods of isolation, the student will be charged with devising his or her own plan for ensuring following of the rules in the future. Isolation will continue until the student has devised such a plan, gotten it approved by the teacher, and made a commitment to follow it.

8. If this does not work, the next step is in-school suspension. Now the student must deal with the principal or someone other than the teacher, but this other person will repeat earlier steps in the sequence and press the student to come up with a plan is acceptable. It is made clear that the student will either return to class and follow reasonable rules in effect there, or continue to be isolated outside of class.

9. If students remain out of control or in in-school suspension, their

parents are called to take them home for the day, and the process is repeated starting the next day.

10. Students who do not respond to the previous steps should be removed from school and referred to another agency.

There is little systematic reasearch available on the strategies described in this section. Survey data reported by Glasser (1977) indicate that implementation of his program has been associated with reductions in referral to the office, fighting, and suspension. But neither his program nor any of the others described here has yet been evaluated systematically to the degree that behavior modification approaches have been evaluated. In part, this is because many of these approaches are new, so that many teachers have not yet heard of them and very few have received specific training in them.

This was shown clearly in a study by Brophy and Rohrkemper (1981), who observed and interviewed 44 teachers working in the innercity schools of a large metropolitan school system and 54 teachers working in more heterogeneous schools in a smaller city. All of the teachers had had at least three years of experience (most had 10 or more). Half were nominated by their principals as outstanding at dealing with problem students, and half as average in this regard.

Few of these teachers had had significant preservice or inservice training in how to manage classrooms or cope with problem students, so most of them had to learn from other teachers and from their own experience. Although many were quite successful, many were not, and even most of those who were successful relied on an unsystematic "bag of tricks" approach developed through experience and had problems articulating exactly what they did and why they did it. Gordon's notion of problem ownership proved useful in predicting the responses of these teachers to various classroom problems, in that most teachers responded with sympathy and attempts to help students who presented student-owned problems but reacted unsympathetically and often punitively to students who presented teacher-owned problems. Few teachers were aware of the term "problem ownership" or of Gordon's suggestions for handling classroom conflicts, however, and even fewer used the problem ownership concept in conjunction with the problem-solving methods that Gordon suggests.

Teachers' responses to interviews about general strategies for dealing with various types of problem students, along with their specific descriptions of how they would respond to vignettes depicting problems that such students typically cause in the classroom, did show some consistent correlations with principals' and observers' ratings of teacher effectiveness in dealing with problem students.

One basic factor was willingness to assume responsibility. Teachers rated as effective made some attempt to deal with the problem personally, whereas teachers rated ineffective often disclaimed responsibility or competence to deal with the problem and attempted to refer it to the principal or someone else (counselor, social worker). Effective teachers often involved these other professionals as *part* of their attempt to deal with the problem, but they remained involved personally and did not try to turn over the entire problem to others, as the ineffective teachers did.

The second general difference was that the effective teachers used long-term, solution-oriented approaches to problems, whereas the ineffective teachers stressed short-term desist/control responses. Effective teachers would check to see if symptomatic behavior was being caused by underlying personal problems (including home problems) and, if so, what might be done about these underlying problems. If they suspected students were acting impulsively or lacked sufficient awareness of their own behavior and its effects on others, they would call for socialization of these students designed to provide them with needed information and insights. If they were behavioristically oriented, they would consider offering incentives, negotiating contracts, or devising other ways to call attention to and reinforce desirable behavior. If they were more insight oriented, they would call for spending time with problem students individually, attempting to instruct and inform them, getting to know them better personally, and fostering insight with techniques much like Gordon's active listening. If they had more of a self-concept/personal adjustment orientation, they would speak of encouraging discouraged students, building self-esteem by arranging for and calling attention to success experiences, improving peer relationships, and so on. All of these various approaches seemed to be more successful than rejecting, punitive approaches, or approaches limited to controlling troublesome behavior in the immediate situation without attempting to deal with larger underlying problems. None of the apparently effective approaches, however, seemed clearly superior to the others in every respect. In fact, a follow up study (Rohrkemper, 1981) comparing teachers who used behavior modification approaches successfully with teachers who used induction (insight oriented) approaches successfully suggested that each approach has its own (desirable) effects, so that a combined approach would be better than an emphasis on one to the exclusion of the other.

Context Differences

So far, this chapter has been written as if principles of effective classroom organization and management were identical for all teachers and settings. To an extent, this is true. Advanced planning and preparation, clarity about rules, routines, and procedures, care in installing these at the beginning of the year and following up thereafter, and regular use of group management techniques are important in any classroom. So is the teacher's willingness to assume responsibility for exercising authority and socializing students by communicating expectations, providing instruction, stimulating insight, helping students to set and pursue goals, resolving conflicts, and solving problems. A great deal of classroom based research is available to guide teachers in developing many of these skills, and a consensus of opinion is available to support most of the rest. Thus, an internally consistent, mutually supportive collection of ideas and techniques is now available for training teachers in effective classroom management.

There still is much room for individual differences, however. For example, although it is important that students become clear about classroom rules and expectations, teachers can follow their own preferences regarding how these rules are determined (on a continuum from teacher as the sole authority who propounds the rules to the students to a democratic approach in which rules are adopted by majority vote at class meetings). Similarly, classrooms can be managed quite nicely without reliance on contingent reinforcement, but there is no reason why teachers who enjoy or believe in rewarding their students for good performance should not do so (although the principles outlined in Figure 1 should be kept in mind). As another example, it seems to be important that students have clear options available to them when they finish their assigned work, and that they learn to follow expectations concerning these options. But what these options are will be determined mostly by teacher preferences and beliefs about what is important. (Options may all require staying in seat or may involve moving to various learning or enrichment centers, for example, and options may differ in the degree to which they are required vs. optional or subject matter related vs. recreational.)

In addition to these differences relating to teacher preference, there will be differences in what is appropriate for different classes of students. Brophy and Evertson (1978) identified four general stages of student intellectual and social development that have implications for classroom management:

Stage One (kindergarten through grade 2 or 3): Most children are compliant and oriented toward conforming to and pleasing their teachers, but they need to be socialized into the student role. They require a great deal of formal instruction, not only in rules and expectations, but in classroom procedures and routines.

Stage Two (grades 2-3 through grades 5-6): Students have learned most of what they need to know about school rules and routines, and most remain oriented toward obeying and pleasing their teachers. Consequently, less time needs to be devoted to classroom management at the beginning of the year, and less cuing, reminding, and instructing are required thereafter.

Stage Three (grades 5-6 through grades 9-10): Students enter adolescence and become less oriented toward pleasing teachers and more oriented toward pleasing peers. Many become resentful or at least questioning of authority, and disruptions due to attention seeking, humorous remarks, and adolescent horseplay become common. Classroom management once again becomes more time consuming, but in contrast to Stage One, the task facing teachers is not so much one of instructing willing but ignorant students about what to do as it is motivating or controlling students who know what to do but are not always willing to do it. Also, individual counseling becomes more prominent, as the relative quiet and stability that most students show in the middle grades give way to the adjustment problems of adolescence.

Stage Four (after grades 9-10): Most students become more personally settled and more oriented toward academic learning again. As in Stage Two, classroom management requires less teacher time and trouble, and classrooms take on a more business-like, academic focus.

Note that these grade level differences in classroom management are more in how much effort is needed and in degree of emphasis given to various classroom management tasks, and not in the underlying principles. This seems to be the case with regard to other individual and group differences in students, as well. At any given grade level, the same basic classroom management principles and strategies seem to apply for boys as well as girls, blacks as well as whites, and for students of various ethnic and social class groups. Physically handicapped students being mainstreamed into regular classrooms may require special arrangements or assistance (see Good and Brophy, 1980, chapter 24), but this will be in addition to rather than instead of the principles described here. Similarly, these principles apply as well to students labeled emotionally disturbed as to other students (Kounin and Obradovic, 1968), although the disturbed students may need more individualized attention and closer monitoring.

Within limits, some adaptation to local expectations or common practice is appropriate. For example, middle-class teachers typically expect students to maintain eye contact with them during disciplinary contacts, as a sign of both attention and respect. However, individuals in certain minority groups are taught to avert their eyes in such situations, and for them, maintaining eye contact may even connote defiance. Obviously, it is important for teachers working with such individuals to be aware of these cultural differences so as to be able to interpret their students' behavior correctly and respond to it appropriately. Similarly, such teachers need to be especially sensitive about avoiding unnecessary conflicts between themselves and their students. For example, student monitor roles should be confined to those that will not place students in conflict with the peer group, and appointments to peer leadership positions will require the involvement or at least the support of the existing peer leaders (Roberts, 1970; Riessman, 1962). In general, it seems important for teachers of any background and in any setting to be openminded and tolerant in dealing with students who come from very different social or cultural backgrounds.

This does not necessarily mean catering to student preferences or automatically reinforcing their expectations, however. For example, middle-class teachers accustomed to forbidding violence in connection with conflicts and forbidding language that they consider to be obscene tend to become noticeably more tolerant of these behaviors if they are assigned to work with lower class students, presumably in deference to local mores (Weiss and Weiss, 1975). Yet, Brookover and others (1979) have shown that schools that are most effective with lower-class students propound and enforce standards for conduct and academic performance, and interviews with students regularly reveal that they are concerned about safety and that they expect and desire their teachers to enforce standards of conduct in the classroom (Metz, 1978; Nash, 1976). Thus, certain behavior should not be accepted even if it is common in the area in which the school is located.

As another example, many students from low socioeconomic status backgrounds are accustomed to authoritarian or even brutal treatment at home, but this is not what they need from their teachers. If anything, these students have a greater need for, and respond more positively to, teacher acceptance and warmth (Brophy and Evertson, 1976). Specifically in the case of minority group students who are alienated from school learning and discriminated against by the majority of the student body, successful teaching involves a combination of warmth with determination in demanding achievement efforts and enforcing conduct limits (Kleinfeld, 1975).

In general, then, the overall goals of classroom management for various categories of special students will be the same as they are for more typical students, although the specific methods used to accomplish these goals may differ somewhat. Distractible students may need study carrels or other quiet places to work, very slow students may need special tutoring and opportunities to get more frequent and personal help from the teacher; and poor workers may need contracts or other approaches that provide a record of progress, break tasks into smaller segments, or provide for more individualized reinforcement.

Conclusion

A comprehensive approach to classroom management must include attention to relevant student characteristics and individual differences, preparation of the classroom as an effective learning environment, organization of instruction and support activities to maximize student engagement in productive tasks, development of a workable set of housekeeping procedures and conduct rules, techniques of group management during active instruction, techniques of motivating and shaping desired behavior, techniques of resolving conflict and dealing with students' personal adjustment problems, and orchestration of all these elements into an internally consistent and effective system. Clearly, no single source or approach treats all of these elements comprehensively.

However, the elements for a systematic approach to classroom management can be gleaned from various sources (particularly recent and research based sources) that provide complementary suggestions. The research of Kounin and his colleagues and of Evertson, Emmer, Anderson, and their colleagues has provided extremely detailed information on how teachers can organize their classrooms, launch the year, and manage the classrooms on an everyday basis. There is less research support for suggestions about counseling individual students and resolving conflicts, but the approaches of cognitive behavior modifiers, Dreikurs, Glasser, Good and Brophy, Gordon, and Morse, among others, implicitly agree on a common set of principles. These include respect for student individuality and tolerance for individual differences, willingness to try to understand and assist students with special needs or problems, reliance on instruction and persuasion rather than power assertion, and humanistic values generally. However, they also recognize that students have responsibilities along with their rights, and that they will have to suffer the consequences if they persist in failing to fulfill those responsibilities. These ideas appear to mesh nicely with the evolving role of the teacher as a professional with particular expertise and specific but limited responsibilities to students and their parents, and with certain rights as the instructional leaders and authority figures in the classroom.

References

Aronson, Elliot; Blaney, Nancy; Stephan, Cookie; Sikes, Jev; and Snapp, Matthew. *The Jigsaw Classroom.* Beverly Hills, Calif.: Sage, 1978.

Brookover, Wilbur; Beady, Charles; Flood, Patricia; Schweitzer, John; and Wisenbaker, Joe. *School Social Systems and Student Achievement: Schools Can Make a Difference.* New York: Bergin, 1979.

Brophy, Jere. "Teacher Praise: A Functional Analysis." *Review of Educational Research* 51 (1981): 5-32.

Brophy, Jere, and Evertson, Carolyn. "Context Variables in Teaching." *Educational Psychologist* 12 (1978): 310-316.

Brophy, Jere, and Evertson, Carolyn. *Learning From Teaching: A Developmental Perspective*. Boston: Allyn and Bacon, 1976.

Brophy, Jere, and Rohrkemper, Mary. "The Influence of Problem Ownership on Teachers' Perceptions Of and Strategies For Coping With Problem Students." *Journal of Educational Psychology* 73 (1981): 295-311.

Camp, Bonnie, and Bash, Mary Ann. *Think Aloud: Increasing Social and Cognitive Skills—A Problem-Solving Program for Children, Primary Level*. Champaign, Ill.: Research Press, 1981.

Cartledge, Gwendolyn, and Milburn, JoAnne. "The Case for Teaching Social Skills in the Classroom: A Review." *Review of Educational Research* 48 (1978): 133-156.

Dreikurs, Rudolph. *Psychology in the Classroom: A Manual for Teachers*. 2nd ed. New York: Harper and Row, 1968.

Emery, R., and Marholin, D. "An Applied Behavior Analysis of Delinquency: The Irrelevancy of Relevant Behavior." *American Psychologist* 32 (1977): 860-873.

Glasser, William. *Schools Without Failure*. New York: Harper and Row, 1969.

Glasser, William. "Ten Steps to Good Discipline." *Today's Education* 66 (November-December 1977): 61-63.

Glynn, E.; Thomas, J.; and Shee, S. "Behavioral Self-Control of On-Task Behavior in an Elementary Classroom." *Journal of Applied Behavior Analysis* 6 (1973): 105-113.

Good, Thomas, and Brophy, Jere. *Looking in Classrooms*. 2nd ed. New York: Harper and Row, 1978.

Good, Thomas, and Brophy, Jere. *Educational Psychology: A Realistic Approach*. 2nd ed. New York: Holt, Rinehart and Winston, 1980.

Gordon, Thomas. *T.E.T. Teacher Effectiveness Training*. New York: David McKay, 1974.

Johnson, David, and Johnson, Roger. *Learning Together and Alone*. Englewood Cliffs, N.J.: Prentice-Hall, 1975.

Kazdin, Alan. *The Token Economy: A Review and Evaluation*. New York: Plenum, 1977.

Kleinfeld, Judith. "Effective Teachers of Indian and Eskimo Students." *School Review* 83 (1975): 301-344.

Kounin, Jacob. *Discipline and Group Management in Classrooms*. New York: Holt, Rinehart and Winston, 1970.

Kounin, Jacob, and Obradovic, Sylvia. "Managing Emotionally Disturbed Children in Regular Classrooms: A Replication and Extension." *Journal of Special Education* 2 (1968): 129-135.

Lepper, Mark, and Greene, David, eds. *The Hidden Costs of Reward: New Perspectives on the Psychology of Human Motivation*. Hillsdale, N.J.: Erlbaum, 1978.

McLaughlin, T. F. "Self-Control in the Classroom." *Review of Educational Research* 46 (1976): 631-663.

Meichenbaum, Donald. *Cognitive-Behavior Modification*. New York: Plenum, 1977.

Meichenbaum, Donald, and Goodman, J. "Training Impulsive Children to Talk to Themselves." *Journal of Abnormal Psychology* 77 (1971): 115-126.

Morse, William. "Worksheet on Life Space Interviewing for Teachers." In *Conflict in the Classroom: The Education of Children with Problems*. 2nd ed. Edited by N. Long, W. Morse, and R. Newman. Belmont, Calif.: Wadsworth, 1971.

Krumboltz, J., and Krumboltz, H. *Changing Children's Behavior*. Englewood Cliffs, N.J.: Prentice-Hall, 1972.

Metz, Mary. *Classrooms and Corridors*. Berkeley, Calif.: University of California Press, 1978.

Nash, Roy. "Pupils' Expectations of Their Teachers." In *Explorations in Classroom Observation*. Edited by M. Stubbs and S. Delamont. New York: Wiley, 1976.

O'Leary, Susan, and Dubey, Dennis. "Applications of Self-Control Procedures by Children: A Review." *Journal of Applied Behavior Analysis* 12 (1979): 449-465.

O'Leary, K. Daniel, and O'Leary, Susan, eds. *Classroom Management: The Successful Use of Behavior Modification*. 2nd ed. New York: Pergamon, 1977.

Riessman, Frank. *The Culturally Deprived Child*. New York: Harper and Row, 1962.

Roberts, Joan. *Scene of the Battle: Group Behavior in Urban Classrooms*. New York: Doubleday, 1970.

Robin, A.; Schneider, M.; and Dolnick, M. "The Turtle Technique: An Extended Case Study of Self-Control in the Classroom." *Psychology in the Schools* 13 (1976): 449-453.

Rohrkemper, Mary. "Classroom Perspectives Study: An Investigation of Differential Perceptions of Classroom Events." Ph.D. dissertation, Michigan State University, 1981.

Rosenbaum, Michael, and Drabman, Ronald. "Self-Control Training in the Classroom: A Review and Critique." *Journal of Applied Behavior Analysis* 12 (1979): 467-485.

Rosswork, Sandra. "Goal-Setting: The Effects on an Academic Task with Varying Magnitudes of Incentive." *Journal of Educational Psychology* 69 (1977): 710-715.

Safer, D., and Allen, R. *Hyperactive Children: Diagnosis and Management*. Baltimore: University Park Press, 1976.

Sagotsky, Gerald; Patterson, Charlotte; and Lepper, Mark. "Training Children's Self-Control: A Field Experiment in Self-Monitoring and Goal-Setting in the Classroom." *Journal of Experimental Child Psychology* 25 (1978): 242-253.

Sharan, Shlomo. "Cooperative Learning in Small Groups: Recent Methods and Effects on Achievement, Attitudes, and Ethnic Relations." *Review of Educational Research* 50 (1980): 241-271.

Slavin, Robert. "Cooperative Learning." *Review of Educational Research* 50 (1980): 315-342.

Stanford, Gene. *Developing Effective Classroom Groups: A Practical Guide for Teachers*. New York: Hart, 1977.

Thompson, Marion; Brassell, William; Persons, Scott; Tucker, Richard; and Rollins, Howard. "Contingency Management in the Schools: How Often and How Well Does it Work?" *American Educational Research Journal* 11 (1974): 19-28.

Weiss, M.; and Weiss, P. "Taking Another Look at Teaching: How Lower-Class Children Influence Middle-Class Teachers." Paper presented at the annual meeting of the American Anthropological Association, 1975.

Webb, Noreen. "A Process-Outcome Analysis of Learning in Group and Individual Settings." *Educational Psychologist* 15 (1980): 69-83.

3

Training Teachers to be Effective Classroom Managers

Vernon F. Jones

Dᴜʀɪɴɢ the 1980-81 school year, I left the college setting to serve as a junior high school vice principal in charge of discipline for 900 students. This experience proved to be a stimulating and meaningful catalyst for reinforcing and refocusing my ideas about classroom management.

I was responsible for assisting the staff in implementing and revising a new schoolwide discipline procedure. Many of the concepts outlined in this chapter were highlighted in that project. During the year, I became acutely aware of teachers' strong concerns about discipline problems as well as their tendency to view discipline almost exclusively in terms of student behavior and punishment. As the teachers in the school began to feel support in their struggle with student misbehavior, they became more able and willing to consider their own roles and responsibilities in relation to discipline problems. This led to an increasingly positive, exciting response and to interventions that began to create a school environment conducive to learning and professional job satisfaction.

The Problem

While classroom management has always been a responsibility assigned to the teacher, proficiency in this area has become one of the key ingredients in the ability to teach well. A variety of social factors has contributed to this situation (Bronfenbrenner, 1974, 1977; Jones, 1980; Jones and Jones, 1981). Unfortunately, teachers have been provided few tools for coping with an increasingly heterogeneous student population that displays a variety of disruptive behaviors. Teachers have suffered behind closed doors while academicians and teacher educators have failed to integrate research and theory into a well-conceptualized, practical approach to classroom management. Even when a wealth of resources has combined to address this issue, the ideas and methods that have resulted have too frequently been myopic and mechanistic. While this bandage approach has occasionally managed to plug the dike, teachers have continued to feel confused, frustrated, and inadequate about their ability to create positive, well-managed learning environments.

Teacher frustration concerning discipline matters is widespread. In its 1979 Teacher Opinion Poll, the National Education Association found that 74 percent of the teachers surveyed stated that discipline problems impaired their teaching effectiveness, and 17 percent said their effectiveness was seriously reduced by discipline problems. Forty-five percent of the teachers surveyed indicated their schools had not done nearly enough to help them deal with discipline problems. In a similar survey, the NEA reported that only 14 percent of today's public school teachers have been teaching more than 20 years — half the percentage of 15 years earlier. Furthermore, only a third of the teachers surveyed said they would make the same career choice again. While anxiety associated with management problems is certainly not the only reason teachers leave the profession, it is a significant factor. Classroom discipline has a direct and major influence on what most teachers consider to be the two key aspects of their professional lives: (1) the degree to which students develop personal and cognitive skills, and (2) the extent to which teachers enjoy their work.

Teachers are not alone in their concern. In the period 1969-1981, 12 of 13 Gallup polls reported that Americans view discipline as the most important problem in the schools, a concern echoed by administrators. Duke (1978) reported that school administrators listed discipline as their top concern and stated that more time should be given to resolving this key issue.

Fortunately, the research and literature on classroom management enables educators to provide teachers with a comprehensive and effective approach to management.

The Need for a Comprehensive Approach to Classroom Management

The widespread concern about disruptive student behavior and school districts' desire to help their staffs has led to a proliferation of consultants and programs espousing solutions to the problem. Unfortunately, the vast majority of these programs have stressed rather simplistic, sometimes gimicky cure-alls. Even programs based on solid research and theory have focused on a limited number of the factors that influence student behavior. This situation is not surprising since such programs are easier to package and sell.

This patchwork approach to teacher training has several major short-

1980), school organization (Duke, 1980), and school climate (Robert, 1976; Olivero, 1977). The growing middle school movement is another example of educators seeking to better understand student needs and realizing that improved behavior and increased learning occur in environments that respond sensitively to those needs.

In *Fifteen Thousand Hours,* Rutter and others (1979) provide striking support for an increased emphasis on preventive measures. This study reported major differences in discipline problems between similar schools in London. Factors associated with limited problems included higher teacher expectations for student behavior and work; teachers themselves demonstrating responsible, professional behavior such as being prepared and starting class on time; fairness in adult-student relationships; and frequent praise of students' work. This study emphasizes the increasingly well-supported belief that behavior problems result when students feel alienated from school. The solution to reducing discipline problems involves creating instructional activities and a general school atmosphere that help students experience success and a sense of belonging.

Once teachers have placed the various management approaches in perspective and understand the general methods they must acquire in order to create positive, well-managed learning environments, the next task is to provide them with the specific skills associated with each method.

Specific Management Skills

Educators involved in training teachers must view their role as synthesizing related research and presenting it in terms of specific teacher skills. While teachers need to know that the methods taught them are based on sound research, they are interested in developing specific behaviors that can be comfortably added to their repertoire. I have found certain specific skills to be the key ingredients in training teachers how to consistently create positive learning environments and effectively cope with the limited behavior problems that do arise.

Understanding Students' Personal and Academic Needs

A knowledge of student needs minimizes teachers' confusion about student failure or misbehavior. This in turn decreases the likelihood that teachers will feel personally affronted by these actions, and enhances their willingness and ability to respond productively to student misbehavior. This knowledge offers teachers hope since it suggests that learning can occur and behavior problems can be reduced if students' needs are met in the classroom. An understanding of student needs serves as the foundation to a diagnostic-prescriptive approach to classroom management.

The theories that seem most useful in explaining student psychological needs include Maslow's (1968) heirarchy of needs, Coopersmith's (1967) antecedents of self-esteem, Erikson's (1963) stages of development, Dreikurs (1971) four mistaken goals, Knopka's (1973) concepts regarding adolescent problems, and Bronfenbrenner's (1974) material on the family. A working knowledge of these theories allows teachers to diagnose possible causes and suggest interventions that will help students meet their needs and subsequently respond more positively.

Teachers' understanding of student academic needs is obviously complex and should include a solid course in cognitive development and learning theory. However, there are several basic concepts that can assist teachers in understanding students' academic behavior. These include the list presented in Figure 3 of ten student academic needs and the idea that commitment to accomplishing a learning goal depends on six factors: (1) how interesting the goal is, (2) how likely it seems that the goal can be accomplished, (3) the degree of challenge, (4) whether the learner can tell if the goal has been achieved, (5) the satisfaction or reward associated with completion, (6) how others relate to the learner throughout the learning process.

Figure 3. Students' Academic Needs

1. To understand the teacher's goals
2. To be actively involved in the learning process
3. To relate subject matter to their own lives
4. To follow their own interests
5. To experience success
6. To receive realistic and immediate feedback
7. To experience an appropriate amount of structure
8. To have time to integrate learning
9. To have positive contact with peers
10. To have instruction matched to their level of cognitive development and learning style (Jones and Jones, 1981, p. 41)

Clarifying Teachers' Beliefs, Values, and Goals

In working with preservice and inservice teacher training, I have been consistently surprised at teachers' inability to articulate a clear statement about human development and learning and its relationship to classroom management. Teachers will be confused by a variety of new skills unless they are able to accommodate them within a clarified professional belief system. An effective program for assisting teachers in developing management skills must provide teachers with structured activities aimed at clarifying their beliefs, values, and goals, and creating a management system consistent with these factors.

Once teachers have developed this foundation, they must be allowed to implement their own management system. I have seen many cases where teachers were immensely frustrated by an administrator's demands that they implement a management system that ran counter to their professional beliefs or style. Mosier and Park (1979) summarize these concerns:

The danger in adopting a set of rigidly established classroom techniques lies in the obvious fact that each teacher also is unique. There is a tendency for any system to become ineffective — a sterile ritual — unless room is made in it for input from the teacher's unique intelligence and personality (xii).

The reason any disciplinary procedure can fail when put into practice is that no procedure is effective if the person utilizing it considers it merely a mechanical means of reaching desired results. Before you adopt the techniques described here — or any other disciplinary system — you must be able to live that system, for its effectiveness necessarily depends on whether it is used superficially or with sincerity (p. 27).

Creating Functional Classroom Norms

As Evertson and Emmer noted in Chapter 1, teachers can significantly reduce management problems by early in the year developing clear rules and expectations and carefully monitoring student responses to them.

It is important that teachers go beyond simply developing a prepackaged set of rules. They must create and consistently reinforce norms that allow for a sensitive response to students' personal and academic needs. In his book *Culture Against Man,* Jules Henry (1963) depicts an example of a destructive classroom norm:

Boris had trouble reducing "12/16" to the lowest terms, and could only get as far as "6/8". The teacher asked him quietly if that was as far as he could reduce it. She suggested he "think." Much heaving up and down and waving of hands by the other children, all frantic to correct him. . . . She then turns to the class and says, "Well, who can tell Boris what the number is?" A forest of hands appears, and the teacher calls Peggy. Peggy says that four may be divided into the numerator and the denominator.

Thus Boris' failure has made it possible for Peggy to succeed; his depression is the price of her exhilaration; his misery the occasion for her rejoicing (pp. 295-296).

A classroom rule that would eliminate this damaging behavior and replace it with a helpful, supportive norm might require everyone to sit quietly while a student answers a question and to assist only if requested.

Since parents can either support or undermine the teacher's values and goals, it is important that teachers develop ways to obtain parental support for classroom norms. This includes creating effective methods for contacting parents early in the year to explain goals and procedures, using parents as resources, and making both positive and critical informative telephone and written contacts with parents.

Employing Effective Teaching Methods

Effective instructional methods and materials are, along with a positive teacher-student relationship, the foundation to effective classroom management. Research suggests that student behavior and learning are heavily influenced by teachers' instructional skills (Brophy and Evertson, 1976; Kounin, 1970; Medley, 1977). Madeline Hunter's Instructional Theory into Practice program also indicates that student learning increases and misbehavior decreases when teachers present well-planned lessons and employ effective instructional strategies. Responding to the growing body of research on the importance of effective instruction, Tanner (1978) wrote:

> The curriculum can be a positive force in classroom control. As a matter of fact the most constructive approach to discipline is through the curriculum. Learning that is interesting and provides a sense of growing power and accomplishment is the best means of classroom control (p. 43).

This sentiment was also voiced by Brophy and Evertson (1976):

> We also found that student engagement in lessons and activities was the key to successful classroom management. The successful teachers ran smooth, well paced lessons with few interruptions, and their students worked consistently at their seatwork (p. 54).

While there are many ways to categorize the instructional skills teachers must possess, Figure 4 presents an outline I have found useful (Jones and Jones, 1981).

Figure 4.

Teaching Strategies That Facilitate Learning and Positive Behavior

Planning Interesting Lessons
Incorporating students' interests
Teaching more than facts
Involving students in the learning process
Responding to students' learning styles

Strategies for Implementing Disruption-Free Lessons
Creatively beginning a lesson
Giving clear instructions
Maintaining attention
Effective pacing
Using seatwork effectively
Summarizing
Making smooth transitions
Providing useful feedback and evaluation
Handling minor disruptions

It is particularly important that the beginning teacher develop these skills since failure to do so can lead to a loss of idealism and commitment, and a subsequent entrenchment in negative behaviors and corrective responses to classroom management.

Establishing Positive Teacher-Student Relationships

The quality of the teacher-student relationship combines with the quality of curriculum and instruction to provide the foundation of classroom management. By the time a child reaches the sixth grade, he or she has spent over 7,000 hours with teachers. The combination of the teachers' expertise, dominance of the classroom, and control over rewards and punishments makes the teacher the dominant figure in the classroom. This causes the quality of the teacher-student relationship to be immensely important in determining whether students experience school as a stimulating and supportive environment. Research indicates that positive teacher-student relationships are associated with positive student attitudes toward school (Fredericks, 1975), increased academic achievement (Aspy, 1972; Berenson, 1971; Kleinfeld, 1975; Rosenshine and Furst, 1973), and more positive behavior (Davidson and Lang, 1960; Truax and Tatum, 1966). William Purkey's book *Inviting School Success* (1978) provides a sensitive and powerful statement concerning the role teacher-student relationships play in influencing student learning and behavior.

Educators involved in training teachers must assist teachers in developing methods for evaluating the current quality of their relationships with students — including the extent to which they may respond differently to various subgroups of students. Teachers must also develop specific sending and receiving skills to respond openly and sensitively to students. Teachers can be taught to improve their rate of positive, supportive comments to all students but particularly to those who are receiving a low rate of these responses. Finally, teachers can be provided with a variety of methods for establishing rapport with students.

Despite the fact that teachers' style of relating to students is an extension of their personal style, it can be altered by systematic data collection and practice. Indeed, most teachers find this to be an exciting and rewarding area for combining personal and professional growth.

Developing Positive Peer Relationships

Anyone who has taught school or served as a school principal or vice-principal is aware of the influence children have on each other. Research verifies the role peers play in influencing classroom learning and behavior

(Coleman, 1966; Schmuck, 1966; Lewis and St. John, 1974). Since many behavior problems involve peer conflict, educators must place greater emphasis on improving peer relationships in school settings. The Positive Alternatives to School Suspensions program (Bailey and Kackley, 1975) has demonstrated that a structured program of humanistic activities in the classroom combined with group counseling in human relations can dramatically reduce acting-out and suspensions in secondary schools.

It is surprising that teachers receive so little training in or reinforcement for implementing classroom activities that enhance positive, supportive, peer relationships. Teachers need assistance in developing a repertoire of acquaintance activities that can reduce tensions, cliques, and inhibitions. Teachers must also be taught skills for developing instructional activities that reinforce cooperation and reduce competition (Johnson and Johnson, 1975). Finally, teachers must be taught to recognize informal norms and peer pressures that are detrimental to student comfort, safety, and learning. When these are recognized they should be met with open dialogue and activities aimed at creating more productive norms and behaviors.

Improving Students' Self-Concepts

No discussion of preventive measures would be complete without a statement about the relationship between students' self-concept and poor academic performance as well as disruptive behavior (Branch and others, 1977; Purkey, 1978). It is important that elementary and middle school teachers develop skills in implementing activities specifically designed to enhance students' self-concepts. These activities support the creation of positive peer relationships and increase the likelihood that students will see the school as a positive, enjoyable place.

The emphasis on developing skills in self-concept activities need not be a focus for training secondary school teachers. Since students' self-concepts are heavily influenced by the quality of teacher-student relationships, peer relationships, and students' academic success, skill in these areas will enhance students' self-concepts without specific self-concept activities in the classroom.

Meeting Teachers' Personal and Professional Needs

Discussions on school management problems have placed far too little emphasis on the quality of life schools provide for teachers. If teachers are to create positive learning environments for students, they must also view school as a positive, supportive atmosphere. Marc Robert (1976) succinctly stated this belief:

. . . no great "humanization" breakthrough between student and teacher will occur unless an organized and concerted effort is made to develop and maintain some realistic human support systems within which staff members can help each other to feel good about their personal and professional effectiveness (p. 44).

Richard and Patricia Schmuck (1974) clarified this issue:

First, the security, comfort, and stimulation that teachers receive from their colleagues increase the amount of personal esteem they bring to interactions with students and the amount of energy they have for working closely with students. Second, staff interactions offer models to students that represent the actual climate of the school (p. 124).

Teacher training obviously cannot create a skill for feeling good at work. However, teachers can be made aware of the central role their own mental health plays in creating positive student attitudes and behaviors. They can learn methods for becoming acquainted with their colleagues, working cooperatively, and providing each other with personal and professional support.

Employing Problem-Solving Methods

It would be nice if preventive measures could eliminate all student misbehavior. However, regardless of how effectively teachers employ these skills, some student misbehavior will occur. Consequently, teachers must develop methods for effectively resolving problems that arise in spite of their best preventive efforts. Unfortunately, teachers have generally lacked the training necessary to help students solve behavior problems (Brown, 1975).

Problem-solving skills are the most important corrective skills teachers can possess. Students at all ages need the security provided by an adult's ability to sensitively, fairly, and competently respond to inappropriate behavior. Furthermore, effective problem-solving skills enable the teacher to listen to students and incorporate student concerns into solutions. Especially when working with adolescents, this involvement is a key factor in reducing tension and increasing students' commitment to a solution (Duke and Perry, 1978; Jones, 1980; McPartland and McDill, 1977). Effective problem solving also serves as a useful model for students of all ages. Tom Gordon (1974) summarized the major advantage of a problem-solving approach:

Teacher-student relationships at the upper-elementary and secondary levels are much more strained and stressful because teachers relied so heavily upon power (backed up by rewards and punishment) when the children were younger. Then, when students are older, they begin to react to these techniques to an ever-increasing degree with anger, hostility, rebellion, resistance, and retaliation. . . . Students do not naturally have to rebel against adults in the schools. But they will rebel against the adults' use of teacher power. Drop the use of teacher power, and much of the student rebellion in schools disappears. (p. 198)

Training teachers in problem-solving skills involves several steps. First, teachers should be informed of the research regarding the impact of various teacher responses to disruptive behavior. For example, research indicates that effective classroom managers scan the classroom and respond to problems before they become major events (Kounin, 1970; Brophy and Evertson, 1976). The same studies suggest the existence of a positive and negative "ripple effect." A negative ripple effect refers to students' reactions to an overly intense or critical teacher response to misbehavior. While this reaction may initially repress the behavior, tension in the class increases and misbehavior may intensify. Conversely, a quiet, immediate intervention can reduce tension and create a positive ripple effect. Once teachers understand the value of certain interventions, they can begin to develop skills in individual and group problem solving. Individual problem solving may involve learning methods such as Glasser's (1965) reality therapy approach or Maple's (1977) shared decision making. Teachers should also be introduced to the ways they can help students resolve their own conflicts. Finally, teachers must have opportunities to develop skills in working with groups to resolve conflicts that involve the entire class. Skill in facilitating a problem-solving class meeting is essential for anyone who plans on working in a school setting.

Implementing Behavioristic Interventions

Teachers are increasingly being asked to work with students who demonstrate rather serious acting-out behaviors. While many of the methods previously described in this chapter will work surprisingly well with these youngsters, the effective classroom manager is equipped with skills for implementing a variety of more structured behavioristic interventions. Teachers should be trained to effectively implement the following behavioristic methods: (1) data collection, (2) systematic social reinforcement, (3) student self-monitoring, (4) individual contingency contracting, and (5) group contingency contracting.

Because behavioristic interventions can be very effective in altering student behavior, there is a tendency for these methods to become the key component in packaged discipline procedures. Teachers need to understand the advantages and disadvantages associated with these methods (Jones,

1980; Jones and Jones, 1981) and learn to use them in association with the numerous teacher skills discussed throughout this chapter.

Working with Parents

By effectively communicating with parents, teachers can increase the likelihood that parents will support desirable student behavior. Parents who believe they are well-informed and who have been consistently treated with respect and concern will often provide valuable assistance not only in altering their child's behavior but also in providing volunteer help, making classroom presentations, and so on. Although the frequency of parent contacts is usually much greater in elementary schools, secondary teachers can also benefit from applying skills in parent interaction. The key skills teachers should develop are: (1) making initial contacts with parents, (2) providing timely information concerning students' academic progress and behavior, (3) holding informative, effective conferences, and (4) productively handling parents' questions and criticism.

Using Resource Personnel

Because there is an increasingly diverse group of students in the regular classroom setting, it is imperative that teachers develop skills in employing personnel and materials to assist them in instructing exceptional children or children who are culturally different from themselves. Teachers should initially be encouraged to consider how their colleagues and administrators can serve as resources. Teachers are often unaware of or fail to use excellent resources available in their own building. Teachers should also understand the roles and availability of educational and psychological specialists in their school district and community. Once teachers are aware of who the resources are, they should learn when to refer and how to provide the referral source with useful data. Finally, teachers should be assisted in developing realistic expectations concerning the services a specialist can provide and the responsibilities the teacher will be expected to take in implementing any recommendations.

Schools have recently begun to provide teachers with support by developing schoolwide discipline procedures. Since many teachers will be involved in developing or working in such programs, they should be introduced to the basic procedures involved in the more popular approaches. Teachers should become aware of the advantages and disadvantages associated with these schoolwide programs. They should also be assisted in developing strategies for incorporating preventive and problem-solving methods in the context of schoolwide programs that are based on corrective, behaviorist approaches.

Teacher Training: When and How

Preservice Training

Teacher training programs must require courses specifically designed to provide students with a comprehensive, skill-oriented approach to discipline. A preservice course has the advantages of (1) providing time for recent learning in educational and developmental psychology to become integrated into an applied approach to student learning and behavior; (2) working with students who have not developed a bias toward classroom management and are thus able to explore it holistically; (3) establishing productive attitudes and skills before lack of skills combine with the demands of teaching to create a negative, control-oriented approach to discipline; and (4) allowing the teacher to enter the classroom equipped to implement effective management methods.

A preservice management course is most effective when offered immediately prior to student-teaching and in association with observation or involvement in a public school classroom. Students' interest is highest when they know they will soon need the skills being developed in the class. Observation or participation in a classroom makes the material concrete while allowing for involvement in data collection and discussions with teachers. However, it is important that the course be taken when students are not responsible for classroom discipline. This enables them to more objectively explore all aspects of discipline rather than focusing on methods for controlling misbehavior.

During a pre-student-teaching course, students must be helped to understand that because they are a guest in someone else's classroom and may enter after the school year has begun, there will be limitations on the methods they can use. Students need assistance in deciding which methods can be effectively and appropriately employed during their student-teaching experience. During their student-teaching, students should attend seminars that provide a forum for them to share their concerns and formalize their philosophy of classroom management in light of their more intensive classroom experiences.

The content of a preservice course should include the material presented in this chapter. However, after receiving an overview of management strategies and student needs, the course should initially focus on the most concrete, observable aspects of classroom management. Specifically, instructional activities dealing with teachers' goals, values, and professional needs are best covered near the end of the course. These activities can be used to help students begin to synthesize the material and develop their own approach to effective classroom management.

Inservice Training

Inservice training is most effective when it begins with an intensive summer session in which teachers can discuss management in a relaxed setting conducive to positive attitudes. Teachers can learn at a time when they are not under pressure to control a specific situation or student. This increases the likelihood that they will focus on all aspects of classroom management. A summer training program also prepares teachers to begin the new school year with a consistent and complete management plan. When taking such a course during the school year, teachers often become frustrated because some of the techniques they learn would have been best employed earlier, while other methods would require changing existing classroom patterns, which might at first disrupt learning. Summer training sessions should be followed by seminars or support group meetings throughout the year. These groups (ideally involving all or most teachers in a building) should meet frequently in the fall to provide support and suggestions as teachers implement new methods.

Inservice training must consistently emphasize practical methods and activities the teacher can use in the fall. Teachers should be assisted in designing specific sequential methods, and in preparing materials for implementing and evaluating these methods. In addition, the summer program should be highly experiential. Whenever possible, teachers should role play methods and take part in activities they plan to use with their students. When hands-on preparation is accompanied by a supportive follow-up seminar, teachers can enjoy exciting success in developing the specific skills so vital to enhancing student success and their own job satisfaction.

References

Aspy, D. "Reaction to Carkhuff's Articles." *Counseling Psychologist* 3 (1972): 35-41.

Bailey, R., and Kackley, J. *Positive Alternatives to School Suspensions*, 1975. Distributed by Pupil Personnel Services Demonstration Project, 1015 Tenth Avenue North, St. Petersburg, Florida.

Berenson, D. "The Effects of Systematic Human Relations Training Upon the Classroom Performance of Elementary School Teachers." *Journal of Research Development in Education* 4 (1971): 70-85.

Branch, C.; Damico, S.; and Purkey, W. "A Comparison Between the Self-Concepts as Learner of Disruptive and Nondisruptive Middle School Students." *The Middle School Journal* 7 (1977): 15-16.

Bronfenbrenner, U. "The Origins of Alienation." *Scientific American* 231 (1974): 53-57.

Bronfenbrenner, U. "Nobody Home: The Erosion of the American Family." *Psychology Today* 10 (May 1977): 40-47.

Brophy, J., and Evertson, C. *Learning From Teaching: A Developmental Perspective.* Boston: Allyn and Bacon, 1976.

Brown, G. "The Training of Teachers for Affective Roles." In *The Seventy-Fourth Yearbook of the National Society for the Study of Education.* Edited by K. Ryan. Chicago: University of Chicago Press, 1975.

Coleman, J. *Equality of Educational Opportunity.* Washington, D.C.: U.S. Department of Health, Education and Welfare, Office of Education, 1966.

Coopersmith, S. *The Antecedents of Self-Esteem.* San Francisco: W. H. Freeman, 1967.

Davidson, H., and Lang, G. "Children's Perceptions of Their Teachers' Feelings Toward Them." *Journal of Experimental Education* 29 (1960): 109-118.

Dreikurs, R.; Grunwald, B.; and Pepper, F. *Maintaining Sanity in the Classroom.* New York: Harper and Row, 1971.

Duke, D. "How Administrators View the Crisis in School Discipline." *Phi Delta Kappan* 59 (1978): 325-330.

Duke, D. *Managing Student Behavior Problems.* New York: Teachers College, Columbia University Press, 1980.

Duke, D., and Perry, C. "Can Alternative Schools Succeed Where Benjamin Spock, Spiro Agnew, and B. F. Skinner Have Failed?" *Adolescence* 13 (1978): 375-392.

Erikson, E. *Childhood and Society.* 2nd ed. New York: Norton, 1963.

Fredericks, B. *Personal Communications.* Unpublished research project. Monmouth, Ore.: Teaching Research, 1975.

Glasser, W. *Reality Therapy.* New York: Harper and Row, 1965.

Gordon, T. *Teacher Effectiveness Training.* New York: Wyden, 1974.

Henry, J. *Culture Against Man.* New York: Random House, 1963.

Hunter, M. "Altering the Alterable Variables." *Educational Forum* 45 (1980): 121-122.

Johnson, D., and Johnson, R. *Learning Together and Alone: Cooperation, Competition and Individualization.* Englewood Cliffs, N.J.: Prentice-Hall, 1975.

Jones, V. *Adolescents With Behavior Problems: Strategies for Teaching, Counseling and Parent Involvement.* Boston: Allyn and Bacon, 1980.

Jones, V., and Jones, L. *Responsible Classroom Discipline: Creating Positive Learning Environments and Solving Problems.* Boston: Allyn and Bacon, 1981.

Kleinfeld, J. "Effective Teachers of Indian and Eskimo Students." *School Review* 83 (1975): 301-344.

Konopka, G. "Requirements for Healthy Development of Adolescent Youth." *Adolescence* 31 (1973): 291-316.

Kounin, J. *Discipline and Group Management in Classrooms.* New York: Holt, Rinehart and Winston, 1970.

Lewis, R., and St. John, N. "Contribution of Cross-Racial Friendship to Minority Group Achievement in Desegregated Classrooms." *Sociometry* 37 (1974): 79-91.

Maple, F. *Shared Decision Making.* Beverly Hills, Calif.: Sage Publishing Co., 1977.

Maslow, A. *Toward a Psychology of Being.* New York: D. Van Nostrand, 1968.

McPartland, J., and McDill, E. "Research on Crime in Schools." In *Violence in Schools.* Edited by J. McPartland and E. McDill. Lexington, Mass.: Lexington Books, 1977.

Medley, D. *Teacher Competence and Teacher Effectiveness, A Review of Process-Product Research.* Washington, D.C.: American Association of Colleges for Teacher Education, 1977.

Mosier, D., and Park, R. *Teacher-Therapist: A Text-Handbook for Teachers of Emotionally Impaired Children.* Santa Monica, Calif.: Goodyear Publishing Company, 1979.

O'Leary, S., and O'Leary, K. "Behavior Modification in the School." In *Handbook of Behavior Modification.* Edited by H. Leitenberg. Englewood Cliffs, N.J.: Prentice-Hall, 1976.

Olivero, J. *Discipline . . . #1 Problem in the Schools? 40 Positive, Preventive Prescriptions for Those Who Care.* Burlington, Calif.: Association of California School Administrators, 1977.

Purkey, W. *Inviting School Success: A Self-Concept Approach to Teaching and Learning.* Belmont, Calif.: Wadsworth, 1978.

Robert, M. *School Morale: The Human Dimension.* Niles, Ill.: Argus Communications, 1976.

Rosenshine, B., and Furst, N. "The Use of Direct Observation to Study Teaching." In *Second Handbook of Research on Teaching.* Edited by R. Travers. Chicago: Rand McNally, 1973.

Rutter, M.; Maughan, B.; Montimore, P.; Ouston, J.; and Smith, A. *Fifteen Thousand Hours.* Cambridge, Mass.: Harvard University Press, 1979.

Schmuck, R. "Some Aspects of Classroom Social Climate." *Psychology in the Schools* 3 (1966): 59-65.

Schmuck, R., and Schmuck, P. *A Humanistic Psychology of Education: Making the School Everybody's House.* Palo Alto, Calif.: National Press Books, 1974.

Tanner, L. *Classroom Discipline for Effective Teaching and Learning.* New York: Holt, Rinehart and Winston, 1978.

Truax, C., and Tatum, C. "An Extension From the Effective Psychotherapeutic Model to Constructive Personality Change in Pre-School Children." *Childhood Education* 42 (1966): 456-462.

Walker, H., and Buckley, N. *Token Reinforcement Techniques: Classroom Applications for the Hard-to-Teach Child.* Eugene, Oreg.: E-P Press, Inc., 1974.

Part Two: Getting Help

4

Meeting Students' Special Needs

Phil C. Robinson and Gail Von Huene

D URING the last two decades, the education profession has seen tremendous growth in its ability to assess and identify students' special needs. While many school districts are experiencing shortages of funds and sharp cut-backs in personnel, it is important to keep in the forefront what we have learned regarding diagnostic procedures and program components appropriate to the special requirements of students. Experience has demonstrated that those requirements sometimes transcend the capacity of the classroom teacher, thus creating the need to reach for outside assistance.

Still, it is the classroom teacher who has primary responsibility for detecting problems that may affect students' academic achievement and adjustment in the school environment. The referral process and system of providing special services rest on the teacher's ability to identify areas of concern and recognition that outside assistance may be warranted. The assessment process itself provides important clues regarding social deficiencies, learning styles, and mental abilities. At the local district level, the complete implementation of P.L. 94-142, perhaps the most comprehensive federal legislation ever enacted, could greatly enhance this assessment process.

One of the difficult problems public school people have had to overcome has been "guess work" in programming for students who do not fit the norm. Since all placement decisions must be made on the best empirical evidence available, objectivity and creative management are vital at each step of the referral process. Maximum objectivity in diagnosing and defining problems can minimize errors in placement, which are not only useless to students but sometimes counterproductive. Misdiagnoses and improper placements have been known to land school districts in court on the losing end of decisions.

The specialized needs of students can present other significant problems for special service personnel, whose tolerance, personal experience, and technical training vary greatly. In order to minimize extraneous input and sharpen the focus of the referral process, some guidelines are necessary. This chapter takes a look at the services that can help administrators working with specialists and classroom teachers. All of the services, procedures, and resources we have identified have proven their usefulness and should be integrated with the guidelines that local districts develop for their own use.

Assessment and Referral

Students who are having difficulty coping with the school environment, due to learning problems other then mental deficiencies, often surface for assessment. Language and cultural differences are sometimes found to be the root cause; often students who are bored show frustration and disruptive behavior. The cries of these students must be answered.

Some student problems are singular in cause and simple to solve, but problems that require outside help are rarely simple. They usually have many contributing factors requiring unique solutions that cannot be provided solely in the classroom.

Specific functions and referral procedures vary from state to state and district to district. Common to all schools, however, is the need to streamline the referral process yet provide as much specific and truly informative data as possible. Establishing systems of recordkeeping can facilitate student referral by making pertinent information easily accessible. Frequency counts, time interval recording, anecdotal records, and work samples gathered over a period of time are always helpful. "He is demanding" tells how the teacher feels. "He is out of his seat daily and talking with others eight to ten times an hour" describes specifically what the student does. Additional notes could describe the student's likes and dislikes, strengths and weaknesses, and what the student will and will not do.

Supervisors and administrators, through observations of students, can assist teachers in making referrals since classroom procedures do not always allow teachers to observe objectively. One study of teacher interactions (Stebbins, 1970) found that teachers use habitual definitions of students' disorderly behavior because they enable split-second interpretations. This is understandable, considering that the typical elementary teacher may engage in 200 to 300 interactive encounters per hour in a working day (Jackson, 1968). Calling in an observer who has credibility in one discipline lends greater objectivity to observations.

The perceptive, well-informed supervisor and building administrator can significantly reduce the time required for implementing the referral process. This requires an awareness of available resources and a knowledge of the nature of the difficulty the student is having.

The first part of solving a problem is defining it. The first step in defining a problem often requires discovering "what is not." For example, hearing may be checked to assure that acuity is not the cause of a student's difficulty in following directions. The second part of defining the problem involves discerning the critical factors contributing to the behavior. All health and physical factors should be checked and ruled out as indicated.

The descriptive terms used to differentiate the technical differences between students with special needs are expansive. The public acts in different states and the rules and regulations also vary. Ancillary and other related services specifically designed to meet the unique needs of handicapped persons through age 21 can be found in all states. The practitioner needs to know the precise linkage between the district, the county, and state-provided ancillary services.

The expression "multidisciplinary evaluation team" has come into common use in recent years. Its current definition refers to a minimum of two persons who are responsible for evaluating a student who is suspected of being handicapped, or re-evaluating a handicapped student for possible reassignment. Such a team should include at least one special education-approved teacher or other specialist with knowledge in the area of the suspected disability. The multidisciplinary evaluation team should also use a checklist to cover all of the factors that may affect the student's condition, such as the student's inability to achieve commensurate with mental ability, extended unhappiness and depression, emotional development, academic history, and adaptive behavior.

When the team has completed diagnostic evaluation, including recommendation of eligibility, then what? It is at this point in the process that the Individualized Educational Plan (IEP) is made. It is also at this point that the teacher, parents, administrators, and members of the Educational Planning and Placement Committee (EPPC) share common information and agree on common goals. The scope of the information that is shared by persons participating in the EPPC is drawn from a variety of sources. Parents' input, aptitude and achievement tests, teacher recommendations, physical factors, social and cultural background, adaptive behavior, and other pertinent data are all considered before a definite IEP is established.

Preventing Follow-Through and Feedback Problems

The person who makes the initial referral should receive early assurance that the referral has been received. When referrals are hand-delivered, they should be revised, dated, and moved to the next step in the process. The next step might be requesting a conference, establishing a time for observation, or scheduling tests or other procedures.

The preliminary results might be shared with the referring party. This step is especially helpful when there is likely to be a time lag between initial assessment and the establishment of an action plan for service. For example, preliminary results might indicate that (1) the student should remain in the present environment with no external aid; (2) the student should be moved to a modified environment with no regular outside resource involvement; or (3) further assessment and workup is necessary if the case is more complicated.

Professional contact should be made with resources outside of the school system. Persons who are responsible for coordinating services and outside referrals will find that an established network of coordinated services can greatly enhance the efficiency of the referral process.

Personnel Resources

The responsibility for organizing and coordinating all available aids and resources usually falls to the building administrator. In some cases, a director of special services assumes or shares the responsibility. Interdisciplinary sharing is a critical element in the effective identification of the problem and in assuring that students' needs are met.

A variety of academic specialists have been identified to help teachers work with these students. They include, but are not limited to, bilingual teachers and teachers of the gifted, general curriculum consultants, and reading and math specialists. The use of reading and math specialists was greatly expanded under Title I. County and state consultants are also used sometimes to supplement local staffs in meeting specific needs.

Involvement of media specialists is an emerging, promising practice. If properly integrated as a member of the Educational Program and Planning Committee, the media specialist/librarian can be a valuable resource for films, books, brochures, magazines, and other materials that can aid the classroom teacher and special education staff. Making sure the media specialist/librarian is aware of students' academic, vocational, special adjustment, language, and other special needs can ensure the staff member's maximum resourcefulness.

A public health nurse or the school nurse is the key person in the resolution of health related problems. In addition to providing certain technical services, a nurse is helpful in giving advice and counsel to students, parents, and teachers. The nurse is able to establish linkage through referrals of students and parents to appropriate doctors, clinics, and other health agencies.

The involvement of parents in the school life of their children is also an important resource that must not be overlooked. Perceptive school personnel can quickly identify those parents who may be directly involved as a positive resource.

The American public is becoming increasingly legalistic in seeking relief from school decisions with which they do not agree. At times, law enforcement and juvenile authorities become involved in problems that have a legal twist and which may need social and medical services as well. The principal, psychologist, social worker, school nurse, school attorney, and other resource persons needs to work in harmony to assure the well-being of minors.

Special Services

Special Education

Many special education students may have either primary or secondary social/emotional problems as well as difficulties in learning that require special educational services. Services for the handicapped as specified in P.L. 94-142 guarantee nondiscriminatory assessment, a free and appropriate education in the least restrictive environment, and individual educational programs for handicapped students from three to 21 years of age in most states. This law places a heavy responsibility on the public schools. Handicapped students make up approximately 12 percent of any normal school age population (more than eight million students in the U.S.) and include the following: the mentally retarded, hard of hearing, deaf, speech impaired, visually handicapped, seriously emotionally disturbed, orthopedically impaired, other health impaired, deaf-blind, multiple handicapped, and the learning disabled. Most states have chosen to follow federal mandates and are guaranteeing diagnostic workups, classroom consultation, and a variety of special services.

Language as a Problem

There are two categories of students with special language needs: students who speak a dialect, and students who are non-English speaking. When their special language needs are not met, these students become frustrated and their academic achievement and social adjustment becomes less than optimum. The teacher's sensitivity to the nature of the problem is the key factor in resolving it. Both groups of students should be provided tutorial services whenever possible.

Vocational Education

Students who are not motivated in standard classrooms or who need a "hands on" approach may benefit from referral to a vocational education specialist. Working in a real job provides opportunities for the development of responsibility and self-confidence. These programs attempt to help students realize their maximum potential by equipping them with skills essential to the modern labor market. Vocational education often includes assessing career aptitude and interest, skill training, aid in developing sound work habits, and firsthand knowledge about the work world. Counseling concerning employment alternatives, training in applying for a job, and learning to get along with fellow workers are all elements of a well-planned program.

Child Abuse

Child abuse has surfaced as a pervasive problem. A child who is being abused may be a behavior problem at school but too afraid to report what is happening in the home. Responsible legal agencies cannot act if school personnel who suspect child abuse do not report it. Child abuse includes injury inflicted to a minor by other than accidental means, such as emotional assault, emotional deprivation, physical neglect, and sexual exploitation. In some states, the teacher is directly responsible for reporting suspected abuse to the authorities. In other states child abuse is reported by the administrator, social worker, or other designated personnel. Each incident with legal implications requires skillful documentation prior to allegation.

Other Problem Areas

Violence and crime, status offenders, and drug abuse are all problem areas that tend to plague the school climate. When any of these offenses are present in the student's life, teaching and learning are adversely affected.

Truancy and dropping out are continuous and growing problems, particularly among older students. The existence of laws is obviously not sufficient to solve the problem. Some school districts have successfully alleviated the problem by initiating alternative attendance schedules. For instance, a student who is needed at home part of the day or who wants to earn extra money and holds a part-time job could be given a schedule for attending required courses for several hours either in the morning or afternoon, allowing the student to forego study halls or nonrequired electives.

Chronic illnesses and recurring diseases also frequently require the use of resources beyond the school. Students with medical problems may give signals of trouble by absenteeism, inattentiveness, unusual emotional reactions, inability to digest food, and frequent requests to use the bathroom. Resolving health related problems can greatly increase a student's level of learning.

Summary

A desire to keep students in school and have them succeed has undergirded the growth and development of special resources. The principle of equal access and the awareness that many young persons were passing through schools without successfully developing their full potential provided the challenge. The focus of this chapter has been on those services that have emerged over a long period of time.

It is understood that many school districts do not have all of these services. Local administrative staffs and resource personnel, however, have an obligation to utilize all available resources inside and outside of the system.

It is important to remember that the learning and adjustment problems faced by young people are complex. They range from minor complications to those that are intricate, pervasive, and clearly beyond the capacity of public school services. An interface with community resources is necessary.

The well-trained classroom teacher with a positive attitude is the priceless resource most needed. Circumstances frequently necessitate that resource professionals assume multiple roles. In any case, care must be taken to minimize diagnostic error and to ensure appropriate placement and educational program goals.

References

Benedetti, Eugene. *California School Law*. Monterey Park, Calif.: Bonanza Publishers, 1979.

Bloom, B. S., *Human Characteristics and School Learning*. New York: McGraw-Hill, 1976.

D'evelyn, Katherine. *Meeting Children's Emotional Needs: A Guide for Teachers*. Englewood Cliffs, N.J.: Prentice Hall, Inc., 157.

Jackson, Phillip W. *Life in Classrooms*. New York: Holt, Rinehart and Winston, 1968.

Lerner, Janet W. *Children with Learning Disabilities: Theories, Diagnoses, and Teaching Strategies*. Boston: Houghton Mifflin Co., 1971.

Michigan Special Education Rules, as Amended August 13, 1980. Lansing: Michigan Department of Education, 1980.

National Society for the Study of Education. *From Youth to Constructive Adult Life: The Role of the Public School*. Edited by Ralph Tyler. Berkeley, Calif.: McCrutchan Publishing Corporation, 1978.

Stebbins, Robert A. *Sociology of Education* 44 (Spring 1970): 217-236.

Waugh, Kenneth W., and Bush, Wilma Jo. *Diagnosing Learning Disorders*. Columbus, Ohio: Charles Merrill Publishing Co., 1971.

5

Teacher Self-Assessment

Mary M. Rohrkemper

I N the past decade, researchers have repeatedly been struck with the sheer complexity of classroom processes. The magnitude of the teacher's task has influenced research questions, methods and models, and affected the very language researchers use to describe classroom phenomena. For example, Kounin's (1970) description of successful teacher management behaviors includes constructs of "withitness," "overlappingness," "account-ability," and "momentum." Doyle (1977) discusses the environmental press of classrooms with the concepts of "multi-dimensionality," "simul-taneity," "immediacy," "unpredictability," and "history." Shavelson (1976) examines teachers' decision making using "preactive" and "interactive" distinctions. As these examples from a range of perspectives illustrate, the classroom is a complex environment within which the teacher not only manages groups, but makes decisions about and interacts with individuals as well (Jackson, 1968).

The recognition that the teacher's task approaches the outer limits of the possible, while intriguing to researchers, is of little use to teachers. The recognition of the need for specific knowledge, strategies, and routines that teachers can implement to reconstruct the classroom "problem space" (Simon, 1969) to reduce it to a manageable task, and to help teachers move optimally within its constraints, is evident in the work of Kounin (1970), Anderson and others (1979), and Stallings and others (1979). (See also Evertson and Emmer, Chapter 1 in this volume.) These researchers address practitioners' needs in terms of techniques teachers can use to prevent

Preparation of this chapter was supported by the Institute for Research on Teaching, College of Education, Michigan State University (Contract No. 400-76-0073). The Institute for Research on Teaching is funded primarily by the Teaching Division of the National Institute of Education, United States Department of Educa-tion. The opinions expressed in this chapter do not necessarily reflect the position, policy, or endorsement of the National Institute of Education.

behavioral disturbances from occurring and to maximize time for instruction. Other related research has been concerned with the restoration of appropriate student behavior (Brophy and Putnam, 1979; Rohrkemper and Brophy, 1979, 1980b). The present discussion encompasses both of these issues in that it deals with the monitoring process that underlies successful classroom management, in terms of both preventing and restoring student behavior. To be effective, teachers should be aware of the fit between their intended and realized strategies and goals. The importance of this awareness and techniques teachers can use to thoughtfully and systematically monitor this link between intention and behavior provide the foci for the present discussion.

Monitoring the effectiveness of intended as well as *un*intended outcomes of a given strategy is often uncomfortable. Self-monitoring involves self-reflection that may bring teachers face to face with motivations, feelings, and actions that are less than professional. Student monitoring may mean hearing that a lesson thought to have gone well didn't, or that a well-meant personal gesture was not understood or appreciated. Careful monitoring, then, requires a certain amount of ego strength and the ability to approach the distance between what is and what is desired with an attitude of challenge rather than defensiveness.

Troublespots

Slippage between intention and action is a pervasive threat to effective teaching. Such slippage is possible in every aspect of teaching, from the more global physical arrangements of the classroom space to specific interactions with individual students. In this section, a few of the more common troublespots that teachers would do well to examine are emphasized.

The Role of Expectations

The Rosenthal and Jacobson (1968) experiment, indicating that teachers' expectations regarding student ability were related to actual student performance, sparked much controversy. Since that initial study, enough research has been conducted to establish that teachers' expectations can—and do—function as self-fulfilling prophesies (Good and Brophy, 1980; Brophy and Good, 1974). As these researchers are careful to point out, however, expectations per se are not inappropriate. What is inappropriate and detrimental to professional behavior is the lack of accuracy and flexibility in these expectations. As Brophy and Good (1974) emphasize, expectations are self-sustaining in that they lead to selective perception (noticing confirming evidence more than disconfirming evidence) and self-serving interpretation (ambiguous evidence is understood in ways consistent with expectations). This combination of selective perception and interpretation gives impetus to a powerful cycle of events leading to self-fulfilling prophecies, in which the teacher's perception/interpretation of students' behavior affects the teacher's behavior. Because students perceive the expectations that teachers hold, their *behavior* also can be affected. The effect of this cycle over time is to perpetuate the original expectations and to mold the students' behavior to fit their teachers' expectations.

Teachers' communication of low or high expectations for student performance have been documented elsewhere (see Good and Brophy 1980; Brophy and Good, 1974; Rist, 1970) and will not be discussed at length here. An important point, however, is that many of the more common ways of communicating low expectations are indirect and subtle and are probably counter to teachers' intentions. For example, while teachers have been found to wait less time for low achievers to answer, demand less from them, and call on them less often than students higher in ability, they likely do so altruistically, to avoid embarrassing or humiliating these students in front of their peers. Thus, while the teacher may move on quickly to get a low ability student "off the spot," the unintended effect is the communication to the student, and to his or her classmates, that the teacher does not expect the student to know the answer no matter how long the wait or how many the hints, and that "not knowing" is at least embarrassing.

As this example illustrates, it is not unusual for teachers (or anyone else) to unintentionally slip into a self-fulfilling prophecy cycle. This is especially the case when one's behavior remains unexamined. Teachers' awareness of their classroom behavior in general, and with specific types of students in particular, is necessary for developing and maintaining appropriate expectations. Maintenance is stressed here because self-monitoring is a continual process. Teachers need to assess their own behavior (*"Am I calling on John enough?" "How much free time is the low reading group able to earn?"*) as well as the effects of their behavior, intended and unexpected, on students (*"Is John beginning to volunteer answers?" "Do the lows and highs play well together at recess?"*).

Implicit in this is the notion that the classroom is dynamic, constantly in flux. Teacher-student relations are reciprocal in that teachers influence students at the same time that students influence teachers (Winne and Marx, 1977). This reciprocal exchange also demands that teachers continuously monitor their own expectations—perceptions, interpretations, and behavior patterns—and those of their students. Teachers need to be aware of how their own behavior and expectations are affected by both student behavior and their more subtle expectations.

The Role of Problem Ownership

Another example of the pervasiveness of expectation effects has been documented in teacher management strategies with students who are difficult to handle in the classroom (Brophy and Rohrkemper, 1981; Rohrkemper and Brophy, 1980a). This interview study with elementary school teachers found that teachers' perceptions of problem students and their subsequent strategies for coping with them formed distinct profiles associated with level of problem ownership.

The notion of problem ownership has its origins in the parenting literature (Gordon, 1970; Stollak, Scholom, Kallman and Saturansky, 1973; Kallman, 1974). Gordon (1974) has suggested that problem ownership also can be examined in the classroom context. Specifically, he suggests that problems in teacher-student interaction can be divided into three types: (1) *teacher-owned problems,* which occur when student behavior interferes with the teacher's meeting his or her own needs or causes the teacher to feel frustrated, irritated, or angry; (2) *teacher-student shared problems,* which occur when the teacher and student interfere with each other's need satisfaction; and (3) *student-owned problems,* which exist separately from and do not tangibly affect the teacher.

The teacher interview data of concern here consisted of teachers' verbatim reports of what they would say and do if each of a series of 24 written vignettes occurred in their classrooms (Brophy and Rohrkemper, 1981). The vignettes depicted 12 types of student problem behavior and represented the three levels of problem ownership.

The findings of this study are limited in that they are based on teacher self-report rather than observed behavior. Nevertheless, they support the data from the parenting and helping behavior literature. Each level of problem ownership produced a different pattern in teachers' perceptions of and attributions about students and, in turn, in teachers' beliefs about the effects they could have on students. These perceptions were associated with distinct strategy profiles across the three levels of problem ownership as well.

The data indicated that making attributions about others' behavior is part of a natural process of making sense of one's social environment. It was also clear that, as in expectation phenomena in general, teachers need to be aware of how their attributions about students affect their beliefs about their own efficacy and their subsequent strategies for coping with these students. While attributional inferences (*"Is she responsible for this?" "Did she act intentionally?" "Is she likely to persist?"*) are probably necessary for accurate diagnosis of a student's behavior, they can become self-defeating. This appears especially likely in teacher-owner problem situations in which a student's behavior threatens the teacher's needs for authority and control. In these situations, the teacher's attributions about the student's capability for self-control (*"Sally had a choice, she could have done otherwise."*), intentions (*"She did this on purpose."*), and likelihood for continued misbehavior (*"She always holds things up when I'm in a hurry."*) were probably correct and, as mentioned earlier, necessary to make an accurate diagnosis of Sally's behavior. It was what followed these attributions that caused problems.

Given these attributional inferences about students like Sally, teachers became pessimistic about their own ability to influence them in meaningful ways. Teachers seemed to adopt a "What's to be done?" type of fatalism that was translated into strategies that were probably doomed before they started.

Thus, when discussing their strategies for someone like Sally, teachers reported restricted communication that did not include instructions about what Sally was supposed to be doing or rationales as to why her present behavior was inappropriate. Teachers' terse demands were linked with punishments and short-term control over Sally, rather than more long-term and pervasive goals. The long-term proactive goals were characteristic of teachers' responses to students presenting teacher-student shared and student-owned problems. The problem-solving approaches in these situations included addressing the possible causes for Sally's behavior (*"Why does she have trouble with my authority? Is it me? Do I lord over her? How does she get along with other adults?"*) or substituting desirable behavior (*"Do I only give her attention when she's misbehaving? How can I arrange for her to get my attention in more positive ways?"*) and are clearly more desirable than the restricted goals that are characteristic of teacher-owned problems.

Thus, while teacher perceptions, expectations and subsequent strategies appeared appropriate in the student-owned and shared problem situations, there was clearly a problem when teachers perceived their authority to be challenged. In these situations, teachers' response patterns were less professional and self-defeating. They were probably also self-fulfilling, so that teachers were involved in the maintenance, if not emergence, of student problem behavior. Here again, teachers need to be aware of ways in which they may unwittingly support behavior patterns among certain students. Teachers need to monitor their own affective reactions to student behavior (*"Why does Tim get under my skin so easily?"*), their assumptions about student intentions (*"Bob does have a reputation, but did he start this, or have I missed something?"*), their own expectations for influencing the student (*"Why do I try harder with Jill than I do with*

Barb?"), as well as their strategies for dealing with difficult students (*"Maybe he doesn't know what I expect him to be doing now?"*).

Self-reflection—including teachers' awareness of their own feelings, intentions, and behavior, and of their students' perceptions of and responses to teacher behavior—is essential if teachers are to realize their goals. Gathering this information, from teachers themselves and from their students, is the key to the monitoring process, both before and after implementing a strategy. Before turning to techniques for gathering perceptual and behavioral information from students, let us examine a final "troublespot"—teachers' use of rewards and praise.

Rewards and Praise

Self-monitoring is no easy process. There are times when more knowledge does not necessarily feel like a good thing or support our favorite theories. This seems especially likely to happen when examining the effectiveness of rewards and praise in the classroom. Teachers, like most of us, enjoy praising and rewarding their students. It is with some skepticism, if not resistance, then, that we read of studies that strongly suggest that rewards and praise can be detrimental to the very outcomes they were designed to achieve (Condry and Chambers, 1978; DeCharms, 1976; Deci, 1976, 1978; Kruglanski, 1978; Lepper and Green, 1978; McGraw, 1978; Pittman and others, 1982; and Brophy, 1981).

Investigations of the effects of rewards on a range of student behavior, including interest, performance (both quality and persistence), learning, and internal locus of control indicate that all appear to be adversely affected by the introduction of rewards and praise *when motivation is already evident*. Thus, when the student is already engaging in the desired behavior, rewards can be counterproductive. Rather than reinforcing the enthusiasm that is present and increasing the students' motivation, the addition of extrinsic factors actually reduces it.

This discussion is confined to conditions where student intrinsic motivation is apparent. Unfortunately, this situation is not typical in classrooms; for whatever reasons, students are often bored or defeated by their work. In many situations, the teacher's task is not so much to maintain motivation as it is to instill motivation where apathy or resignation exist. Rewards per se are not the final answer in these conditions, either; to be effective, rewards must be used judiciously.

Teachers may be helped in the decision of *when* to use rewards by examining the work of McGraw (1978) and Condry and Chambers (1978). McGraw developed a four-celled matrix based on the degree of elaboration required by a task and the task's attractiveness to the learner. He found that student performance on algorithmic tasks (routine, familiar procedures) was not adversely affected by the introduction of rewards. In fact, when students did not particularly like assignments that were repetitious and of a practice nature, rewards enhanced their performance. In contrast, McGraw found that rewards had a detrimental effect on performance when given to students working on tasks that were heuristic. Condry and Chambers bolster this finding. They emphasize that the learning process is different from the learning product (performance), and indicate that the *process* is detrimentally affected by rewards. They argue that effects of rewards differ depending on the extent to which the student has already learned the subject matter. Thus, rewards for tasks already learned (McGraw's algorithms) are *not* detrimental because the process of learning has already occurred and the focus is now on learner production of what he or she knows.

In contrast, the process of learning (McGraw's heuristic) is detrimentally affected by rewards. The performance context created by the reward hampers the learning process because it inhibits the use of heuristics, learning of new skills, and incidental learning—all of which require cognitive risks and exploration and thus do not provide a direct route to the promised reward. The goal of learning in these instances, then, is antithetical to the goal of performance for reward. Taken together, the McGraw and Condry and Chambers findings indicate that rewards are best administered in well learned or algorithmic tasks as opposed to skills that are in the process of being learned or are heuristic in nature. Seatwork performance, which is of a practice nature, is likely to be facilitated by rewards, while rewards for students who are learning a new topic area or reading a story are likely to have a detrimental effect.

Information about the *circumstance and form* of rewards is provided by Deci (1976, 1978), whose research supports the importance of the "type" or the "dual nature" of reward. Rewards can either control one's behavior or give information about one's competence. If a student perceives the teacher's reward as controlling, Deci predicts a decrease in the student's intrinsic motivation. If the student perceives the reward as providing feedback about his or her knowledge or competence, however, an increase in intrinsic motivation is likely.

Deci further distinguishes between two types of reward contingency: "task contingent" and "quality contingent." Task-contingent rewards rest on the mere completion of work, while quality-contingent rewards are associated with the level of excellence of that work. Such quality-contingent rewards enhance motivation because they provide information to the learner about his or her competence. Thus, the teacher who requires students to complete seatwork *correctly* before participating in a desired activity provides students information about their ability to meet the teacher's quality expectations when they earn the activity time. In contrast, a teacher who focuses only on students *completing* seatwork assignments to earn free time provides students with information regarding their compliance to classroom procedures when free time is earned, as opposed to information about their competence.

Finally, work by Lepper and Greene (1978) and Kruglanski (1978) indicate an additional consideration: in order to minimize the perception of "other" control, and enhance students' feelings of self-efficacy, rewards should be subtle. The more salient a reward is, the more apt students are to attribute their efforts to the attainment of the reward, and not to the value of learning the task itself. Rewards, then, are most likely to be effective when they are less salient, convey information on the quality of performance, and are contingent on the quality of the work rather than on mere task engagement or completion. O'Leary and O'Leary (1977) include the notion that praise should be specific (vs. global), credible (vs. contrived), and of the appropriate magnitude. Brophy (1981) adds the notion of infrequency to his discussion of effective praise.

These criteria seem to be useful additions to the above caveats for administering rewards. Thus, the more subtle and specific form of teacher praise—*"John you've gotten nine out of ten problems correct. That's two more than you got right yesterday. Good work!"*—is likely to be more effective than more effusive and global praise—*"John! Great! That's wonderful! Look, class!"*

These rules of thumb reflect current thinking on when and how to use rewards in the classroom. This is only the starting point in reward use, however. In order to meet these criteria, teachers must be aware of how students perceive their teachers' intentions. This notion of students mediating the effects of rewards was implicit in Deci's distinction between informational and controlling rewards, and Kruglanski's and Lepper and Greene's discussion of reward saliency. A reward or praise does not occur in a psychological vacuum; how a student interprets a reward determines whether the reward will have its intended effect. Much has been written on this point (Weiner, 1979; Dweck, 1975; Dweck and Goetz, 1978; Ross, 1976; Brophy, 1981; Morine-Dershimer and Galluzzo, 1980).

Briefly, the attributions that an individual student makes when rewarded for a given performance may differ dramatically across students. Take, for example, a student who has low potential for success in the classroom. After giving the class an assignment to write a story, the teacher monitors the room, commenting on student progress. When she gets to Andy, the teacher sees that he is clearly struggling, with little hope of completing the task. Searching for *something* positive to say to encourage him, she exclaims, "My, Andy, what a neat "m" you made!" Andy starts and blushes as the teacher moves on to other students. It is doubtful that Andy feels praised. In fact, the teacher unwittingly may have communicated to Andy that he is *not* smart and that she feels sorry for him and has little, if any, expectations that he will ever meet grade-level standards. This example underscores the critical role of student mediation of teacher behavior. What many teachers unwittingly communicate to those very students they so much want to support and encourage is a devastating message indeed.

Individual student perceptions need to be taken into account in terms of teacher praise in general. Like Brophy (1981), I suspect strong grade-level differences in students' reception to public praise. Where a first-grade boy may blush with delight that his teacher has singled him out, a fifth-grader may be mortified to hear the teacher announce to the class, "I like the way Susie is all ready for the test!" The effective choosing of the timing, general circumstances, and form of rewards and praise rests on teacher sensitivity to individual student interpretation. This concern for student mediation of teacher reward and praise attempts is but one instance of teachers' general need to monitor students' perceptions of and responses to teacher behavior.

Strategies For Monitoring Students

Even though teachers may carefully examine their *own* intentions and behavior, they cannot assume their students share these perceptions. Because teaching is a social process, accurate communication can only be assured when teachers are aware of their students' understanding of teacher behavior and expectations. Too often teachers assume that students have this understanding when they do not. Students' perceptions become more stable and more disparate over time—so much so that in the spring of the school year when a first-grade student is asked how he knows when he is finished with a seatwork ditto, he responds, "You're done when the teacher doesn't tell you to erase anymore" (Anderson, in progress).

The problem is not only that students do not always understand teacher motivation, but that some students apparently either have little expectation that teacher behavior is *supposed* to make sense, or they misattribute to the teacher attitudes and motives that are counter to mutual trust and support. Careful gathering of information from and about students is a step toward bridging this gap between student and teacher perceptions. There are three methods for obtaining this information, including observation, class discussion, and interview.

Observation

Group monitoring. Observing and interpreting continuous classroom behavior is difficult because of the pace and sheer number of activities. Facing one's "perceptual blinders" (Good and Brophy, 1978) is an important first step toward *learning from* observation rather than merely verifying or justifying one's prior notions. For example, when examining the effectiveness of a reprimand on a student who has been fooling around, the teacher should not look *just* to that student's repeated misbehavior. The teacher also needs to look for effects on the student's classmates who both witness and vicariously experience his reprimand. Do the unlookers appear frightened? Intimidated? Irritated? Has the teacher succeeded in stopping one student at the expense of appearing unfair to the rest of the class, who now wonder if it will happen to them too? Such unintended effects invite divisive coalitions between teacher and students. This concern holds for reinforcement as well. In praising Sally, has the teacher inadvertently portrayed her as the "teacher's pet" and made her a target of ridicule by her peers?

These types of unanticipated ripple effects on classmates and on the target student need to be monitored. Take for example, the case of the "ILTW"—"I like the way Joe is sitting tall and ready to begin."—a favorite strategy of many teachers, designed to get the rest of the class moving in the desired direction. Teachers using this strategy should monitor not only the *intended* effects (does the class get ready?), but also the *un*intended effects on Joe, who may feel used, resentful, or worried about the inevitable banter at his expense during lunch.

Group monitoring helps teachers gauge the full range of effects of their behavior with a single student. It also helps teachers improve their teaching plans, use of discussion, grouping, topic changes, and so on. Subgroups of students or "steering groups" are subsets of students that teachers carefully monitor to help them make these types of lesson pacing and format decisions for the entire class (Lundgren, 1972).

The makeup of this core group of students, like so many other teacher decisions, reflects the teacher's values. For example, teachers who work from more of a mastery model orientation are likely to choose their steering group from students toward the lower end of the continuum. In contrast, teachers who value advancing more gifted students are likely to position the steering group higher up the ability scale. One would expect that such subgroups of students are also monitored by teachers to assess class interest, acceptable levels of noise and movement, and so on. Just as teachers need to be aware of unanticipated group reactions to individual teacher-student exchanges, they also need to be aware of the reactions of non-steering-group students. Are higher ability students underachieving? Are lower ability students becoming frustrated?

Target student monitoring. Closer, more intensive monitoring of specific target students is often needed. The problems of selective perception and self-serving interpretation are serious in these situations, but can be reduced through systematic record keeping. Records should account for the context of student behavior. Under what conditions does the student behave inappropriately: during math seatwork, reading group, discussion, lecture? Teachers should also analyze events that precede the objectionable behavior. Is there a predictable sequence of events? Does it usually occur after lunch, before recess, after making a public mistake, or receiving poor test results? And what are the consequences of the student's behavior? Does the class laugh, is the lesson delayed, does the teacher yell?

In addition to this basic antecedent–behavior–consequence formula, teachers need to consider the student's intentions, as well as the intensity, duration, and generalization of the behavior. How serious is the misbehavior? Is it typical of the student? Does it appear to be intentional? Could the student have done otherwise? How long has he acted this way? Does he act this way anywhere else? Under what conditions does the student act most appropriately? What are the positive aspects of his behavior that could be strengthened? (For a more complete treatment of classroom observation, see Good and Brophy, 1978).

Answers to these questions can lead to hypotheses about the student's behavior. These hypotheses can then be verified, changed, or abandoned through systematic observation of the student on subsequent occasions and in differing contexts. Teacher hypotheses can then be shared with the student, either by interviewing the student *("I notice when you sit near Terry you have difficulty completing your work. I wonder if Terry distracts you or are you having difficulty with the assignment?"),* or less directly through class discussion *("Class, we seem to be having trouble with our seating arrangements. What can we do to help each other get all our work done?").* This verification process is important. Although much is gained from careful observation, it cannot guarantee correct interpretation of what is seen, nor accurate communication of what is expected in lieu of the present situation. Further, the observer is limited by his or her own experience (and expectations), and is less likely to fully understand any unanticipated events.

Observation is important, but it does not stand alone. It provides teachers with data and hypotheses upon which to base class discussion or interview, and to explore students' perceptions of their own behavior as well as their teacher's. Systematic observation followed by discussion has a double benefit in that it not only delves into the student's understand-ings, but it also provides information to teachers as they examine the differences between their hypotheses about the student and the student's self-disclosure. These possible discrepancies shed light on teachers' own expectations for students that may be inappropriate.

Class Discussion

Class discussion can be a powerful method for understanding student perceptions as well as a mechanism for teachers to communicate their goals for the class (Glasser, 1969; Bessell and Palomares, 1967). When handled properly, class discussion enables the teacher and the students to understand that there is no single, objective, and correct perception of events. Students and teachers are exposed to the range of perceptions and the subjective nature of interpersonal understanding.

Class meetings are an especially appropriate vehicle for teachers to learn about *students'* expectations and how the teacher's behavior may or may not be reinforcing these expectations. Just as teachers selectively perceive and interpret phenomena, so also do students. Class discussions can be enlightening experiences for all concerned. In addition, teachers have the opportunity to model for the students an acceptance of diversity, openness to criticism, acknowledgement of responsibility, personal insight, and skills to enhance clear communication of personal intentions and reactions to others.

To be successful, class meetings require good judgment, a strong ego, and the ability to deal with things one may not want to acknowledge, in nonemotional, or at least nonblaming ways. In order for students to feel free to express criticism, beliefs, or doubts, teachers must act in counselor-like roles, not as authority figures. This ability to act as an empathic listener first and an authority figure second is also essential to conducting individual student interviews.

Interviewing Students

Issues. In recent years classroom research has begun to include the notion of "perspective." Researchers have become aware of the limitations of classroom observation techniques and the difficulty in interpreting data in ways that are psychologically meaningful to the participants. "Partici-pants" has more recently been expanded upon to include students, as well as teachers. Thus, interview studies are now likely to involve interviews with both teachers and students. Systematically interviewing students in nonclinical settings to learn about their unique perceptions is a surprisingly recent activity. My general recommendations are based on research efforts to interview children (Cannell and Kahn, 1968; Good, 1981; Weinstein, 1980; Wolf, 1979; and Yarrow, 1960).

First and foremost, the interview is a social process. The relationship between interviewer and interviewee has the potential to assist as well as limit the interview. Teachers' stance as concerned and interested adults, in terms of conducting class discussions, is equally critical to the quality and validity of individual student interview data. Invalidity, the degree to which the information the students provide does *not* reflect their true feelings and thoughts, is a significant problem in interviews. Again, teachers need to examine their biases and expectations and be aware of distortions in student reports that may be elicited by the type of question *("Why did you do that?"* vs. *"Tell me what happened."),* the teacher's manner (blaming, supporting, or neutral), or the presence of consequences the student may wish to obtain (strong teacher approval) or avoid *("You'll miss gym for the week if what Bob said is true. Now, did you . . .?").* Obviously, not all presentation effects can be controlled. When teachers do not feel they can disassociate themselves enough to obtain valid data, it may be wise to ask a colleague or classmate to interview the student. Asking fellow teachers to interview students is, in any case, a good strategy, as is asking them to observe in the classroom. Colleagial evaluation provides an objective professional opinion that usually is helpful and provides information to teachers about themselves and their students.

A related concern is the issue of the reliability of the student's information. That is, would the student provide the same information on subsequent occasions? This issue is perhaps less important than the validity concerns because perceptions are not *static.* One rule of thumb to increase the probability that information is an accurate reflection of the student's thoughts and is consistent on subsequent occasions is to interview students *after* they have "calmed down." That is, once students are removed from the immediacy of a situation it is likely that they will have had time to reflect on their experience, have better insight, and be better equipped to report their perceptions. Their reports are more likely to be reliable after some initial "distancing." However, reliability does not always serve validity. When concerned with how the student feels when *in* a situation, immediacy takes precedence.

The optimal lag between the time of an event and the time it is discussed may vary among students. One constraint is the accessibility of information (Cannell and Kahn, 1968; Ericsson and Simon, 1980; and Nisbett and Wilson, 1977). The student may not have the desired information. If it's been some time since the event happened, the student may have forgotten the details, in which case a simple reminder should help the interview move along. In other instances, the student may have repressed the details to avoid stress, or distorted the event by reconstructing it in his or her memory. Or the student simply may not have the desired information; it was never known in the first place because it was outside the student's experience, vocabulary, or level of sophistication. (This factor is especially relevant when dealing with younger children.) It clearly takes a sensitive interviewer to distinguish the cause for a child's responding, "I don't know," and to follow up appropriately. Within these constraints, however, there is much that can be learned about the effectiveness of instruction, students' understanding of teacher intention and expectations, and students' attitudes toward one another and the teacher, through the careful use of interview.

Techniques. Yarrow (1960) delineates many of the considerations in constructing and conducting interviews. He includes the degree of standardization of the questions (teacher preparation of specific questions vs. general topics), the degree of directiveness of the interviewer's behavior (the teacher maintaining control of what is discussed vs. following the student's leads), and the degree of structure in the questions and in the type of responses that are desired (*"Do you understand why I want you in your seat during art?"* vs. *"How can we be careful not to have accidents?"* vs. *"What are some things we could do so that we can all have a good year?"*).

Yarrow further distinguishes between direct, indirect, and projective questions. While direct questions can elicit factual information, indirect questions are better when more information about complex student attitudes, feelings, and expectations is desired. For example, if a teacher is concerned about a particular student's lack of interest in social studies, the teacher may choose to ask the student indirect questions based on observation of the student's behavior and an analysis of what is involved in a social studies lesson. The teacher might ask: "Of reading, math, and social studies, which do you like most (dislike least)?" And again, "If you could choose to quietly read, have a class discussion, or have me lecture, which would you choose first? What next?" and so on, to narrow down what it *is* about social studies that interferes with the student's work habits. Note that the student was not asked what he *didn't* like. Information concerning his least preferred choice was obtained without the student having to feel that he was complaining or being critical. Note also that the example includes a "backup" question that is prepared *in advance* in case the initial question is not understood or is not relevant to the student's frame of reference. These backup questions, like the original, are also nonemotional and nonjudgmental. Often, it is useful to "concretize" these questions to facilitate student understanding. The benefits of this are especially relevant when interviewing younger students or those who are less verbal.

The advantages of this type of questioning are especially great when asking students about specific people. For example, rather than require a child to say he does *not* like or wish to work with a certain classmate, the teacher can ask instead: "Pretend that _____, _____, and _____ all live in your neighborhood. Who do you think you'd like best? If _____'s sick and can't play, who's house would you go to next?" Or, "If you could choose _____, _____, or _____ to be your partner in reading, who would you like to work with the most? If _____'s sick today, who would you choose to work with next?"

When the teacher feels the student has repressed memory of an event, or has severely distorted his recollections, or is simply leery of being directly critical of the teacher, the teacher can ask projective questions that concern hypothetical situations. For instance, a teacher who is concerned that a low ability student is becoming detached and withdrawn might relate a situation about a fictional student from another class with the same behavior and ask the student, "How do you think he felt in school? How do you feel about him? What about other kids? What do they think?" By using a story, the teacher allows the student to discuss his or her own concerns with less anxiety.

Stories are also useful devices for uncovering how students perceive the teacher's behavior toward and expectations for students. For example, teachers could use the following stories.

"Carl could do good work in school, but he fools around a lot. Carl hardly ever does his assignments when he tells his teacher he will. Today during work time everyone is busy, except Carl. He is making paper airplanes.

"Brian is not very smart in school. Even though Brian tries hard, he has trouble learning things, and lots of times he gets answers wrong. Today the class began new work in math. Everyone was busy except Brian. The teacher asked Brian if something was wrong. He said that he tried, but he couldn't do his work; it was too hard."

Teachers could ask after each story, "Pretend I was Carl's (Brian's) teacher. What would I say if that happened? What would I do?"—followed with, "Why do you think I would do those things? What would I expect Carl (Brian) to do? What would I think about Carl? (Brian?)" In this way, teachers could explore how students perceive their motives, behavior, and expectations for students. Teachers could use this information to help them either correct inaccuracies in students' perceptions or to change their own behavior to make it consistent with their intentions.

Reducing a student's response anxiety can also be achieved by suggesting that others have felt the same way the student does, or by mentioning a variety of feelings or actions that people share, without attaching preference to any. A teacher might ask, "Everybody gets bored sometimes. I've noticed that some kids get bored when the work's too hard, some when it's too easy, others get bored in some classes but not others, some kids only get bored during seatwork. What about you? When do you get bored? Why do you think that is?" The teacher lets the student know that she is aware that everyone gets bored and that it is understandable. By providing a range of possible situations that could be boring, the teacher is more likely to put the student at ease and obtain valid information. (Other techniques useful to reduce student anxiety involve using anonymous questionnaires and surveys. Student responses may be more restricted and confounded with writing ability, but they do afford students an opportunity to "tell it like it is" without fear of retribution. These techniques are also beneficial in that they consume less time and give a quick sense of how the class as a whole perceives a given teacher behavior. Tradeoffs when using these methods include the inability of the teacher to clarify questions, to assure the student of the teacher's concern, or to probe with additional questions if the student's meaning is unclear.)

It is also important to attend to question sequencing when interviewing students. Again, Yarrow (1960) provides useful guidelines, two of which seem especially appropriate for the teacher-student interview. These include being sure that the student can successfully answer the opening question, which sets a positive tone; and saving more difficult and sensitive questions for later in the interview, after confidence and rapport have been established. In addition, in some situations the teacher may want to use the "funnel" sequence, in which the interview proceeds from broad topics to specific questions. The teacher may open a discussion with, "What do you think about school? How is it different from what you expected?" Notice that neither question allows for a simple "yes" or "no" answer. The teacher then restricts the scope of later questions to his or her specific concern.

A few final comments on interviewing individual students. First, teachers should identify the situation and their rationale clearly, so that students understand that the teacher is trying to obtain information and further understanding, and not to punish or moralize. Second, it is important for teachers to establish a credible tone of interest and concern but not one of evaluation or emotional release. Students need to understand their teacher's intentions and to be able to trust them with their perceptions. If students get the impression that all this will come back to haunt them, resistance, face-saving, or ingratiation are apt to occur. The invalid information obtained under these circumstances does little to improve teacher-student relations.

Such then are the guidelines for interviewing students in general. Redl (1966), Morse (1971), and Gordon (1970, 1974) have also developed procedures for interviewing students about specific problem incidents in which they are involved. Briefly, they stress the calm, methodical gathering of information from all participants. Each student has a turn to present his or her "side" without interruption. The teacher's role includes laying the initial ground rules and facilitating the presentation of each student's perspective. Teachers, with the students, then discuss discrepancies in testimonies, and search for ways of handling such incidents in the future. Teachers clearly state their own feelings about *unacceptable* student behavior as well as expectations for *appropriate* student behavior. The key to this approach is the nonpejorative problem-solving behavior of teachers. In the process, the students are encouraged to discuss and explore their own feelings and perspectives while being exposed to others' as well. Teachers report that this method is especially effective when dealing with problems among students (fights, arguments, and so on).

This type of problem-focused interview and interviewing in general can provide teachers with information that will help them better understand the student behavior they observe in their classrooms. Increased understanding should help them "read" their students more accurately in the future, and facilitate monitoring their effects in the classroom.

Summary

In order to realize their goals, teachers need to be sensitive to the fit between their intentions and their behavior; to be aware of the effects of their behavior on students; and to monitor students' perceptions. The guidelines for monitoring these student perceptions include systematic observation, class discussions, and individual interviews to gather information about both the intended and the unintended effects of teacher behavior. In these ways, teachers can obtain information and feedback that will make the classroom experience more fruitful for themselves and their students.

References

Anderson, L. "Student Responses to Classroom Instruction Project." East Lansing, Mich.: Michigan State University, in progress.

Anderson, L.; Evertson, C.; and Brophy, J. "An Experimental Study of Effective Teaching in First Grade Reading Groups." *Elementary School Journal* 79 (1979): 193-223.

Besell, H., and Palomares, U. *Methods in Human Development*. San Diego: Human Development Training Institute, 1967.

Brophy, J. "Teacher Praise: A Functional Analysis." *Review of Educational Research* 51 (1981): 5-32.

Brophy, J., and Good, T. *Teacher-Student Relationships: Causes and Consequences*. New York: Holt, Rinehart and Winston, 1974.

Brophy, J., and Putnam, J. "Classroom Management in the Elementary Grades." In *Classroom Management. The 78th Yearbook of the National Society for the Study of Education, Part II*. Edited by D. L. Duke. Chicago: University of Chicago Press, 1979.

Brophy, J., and Rohrkemper, M. "The Influence of Problem Ownership on Teachers' Perceptions of and Strategies for Coping with Problem Students." *Journal of Educational Psychology* 73 (1981): 295-311.

Cannell, C., and Kahn, R. "Interviewing." In *Handbook of Social Psychology, Vol. 2*. 2nd ed. Edited by G. Lindzey and E. Aronson. Reading, Mass.: Addison-Wesley, 1968.

Condry, J., and Chambers, J. "Intrinsic Motivation and the Process of Learning." In *The Hidden Cost of Rewards: New Perspectives on the Psychology of Human Motivation*. Edited by M. Lepper and D. Greene. New York: Erlbaum, 1978.

DeCharms, R. *Enhancing Motivation: Change in the Classroom*. New York: Irvington, 1976.

Deci, E. L. *Intrinsic Motivation*. New York: Plenum Press, 1976.

Deci, E. L. "Applications of Research on the Effect of Rewards." In *The Hidden Cost of Rewards: New Perspectives on the Psychology of Human Motivation*. Edited by M. Lepper and D. Greene. New York: Erlbaum, 1978.

Doyle, W. "Learning the Classroom Environment: An Ecological Analysis." *Journal of Teacher Education* 28 (1977): 51-55.

Doyle, W. "Making Managerial Decisions in Classrooms." In *Classroom Management. The 78th Annual Yearbook of the National Society for the Study of Education, Part II*. Edited by D. L. Duke. Chicago: University of Chicago Press, 1979.

Dweck, C. "The Role of Expectations and Attributions in the Alleviation of Learned Helplessness." *Journal of Personality and Social Psychology* 31 (1975): 674-685.

Dweck, C., and Goetz, T. "Attributions and Learned Helplessness." In *New Directions in Attributional Research, Vol. II*. Edited by Harvey, Ickes, and Kidd. New York: Erlbaum, 1978.

Elliott, J. "Developing Hypotheses About Classrooms From Teachers' Practical Constructs: An Account of the Work of the Ford Teaching Project." *Interchange* 7 (1976-77): 2-22.

Ericsson, K. A., and Simon, H. A. "Verbal Reports as Data." *Psychological Review* 87 (1980): 215-251.

Glasser, W. *Schools Without Failure*. New York: Harper and Row, 1969.

Good, T. "Listening to Students." Paper presented at the annual meeting of the American Educational Research Association, Los Angeles, 1981.

Good, T., and Brophy, J. *Looking in Classrooms*. 2nd ed. New York: Harper and Row, 1978.

Good, T., and Brophy, J. *Educational Psychology: A Realistic Approach*. 2nd ed. New York: Holt, Rinehart and Winston, 1980.

Gordon, T. *Parent Effectiveness Training*. New York: Wyden, Inc., 1970.

Gordon, T. *Teacher Effectiveness Training*. New York: Wyden, Inc., 1974.

Jackson, P. *Life in Classrooms*. New York: Holt, Rinehart and Winston, 1968.

Kallman, J. R., "A Developmental Study of Children's Perceptions and Fantasies of Maternal Discipline Procedures." Doctoral dissertation, Michigan State University, 1974.

Kounin, J. *Discipline and Group Management in Classrooms.* New York: Holt, Rinehart and Winston, 1970.

Kuglanski, A. "Endogenous Attribution and Extrinsic Motivation." In *The Hidden Cost of Rewards: New Perspectives on the Psychology of Human Motivation.* Edited by M. Lepper and D. Greene. New York: Erlbaum, 1978.

Lepper, M., and Greene, D., eds. *The Hidden Cost of Rewards: New Perspectives on the Psychology of Human Motivation.* New York: Erlbaum, 1978.

Lundgren, U. *Frame Factors and the Teaching Process.* Stockholm, Almqvist and Wiksell, 1972.

McGraw, K. "The Detrimental Effects of Rewards on Performance: A Literature Review and a Prediction Model." In *The Hidden Cost of Rewards: New Perspectives on the Psychology of Human Motivation.* Edited by M. Lepper and D. Greene. New York: Erlbaum, 1978.

Morine-Dershimer, G., and Galluzzo, G. "Pupil Perceptions of Teacher Praise." Paper presented at the annual meeting of the American Educational Research Association, Boston, 1980.

Morse, W. "Worksheet on Life Space Interviewing for Teachers." In *Conflict in the Classroom: The Education of Children With Problems.* 2nd ed. Edited by N. Long, M. Morse, and R. Newman. Belmont, Calif.: Wadsworth, 1971.

Nisbett, R., and Wilson, T. "Telling More Than We Can Know: Verbal Reports on Mental Processes." *Psychological Review* 84 (1977): 231-259.

O'Leary, K., and O'Leary, S., eds. *Classroom Management: The Successful Use of Behavior Modification.* 2nd ed. New York: Pergamon Press, 1977.

Pittman, T.; Boggiano, A.; and Ruble, D. "Intrinsic and Extrinsic Motivational Orientations: Limiting Conditions on the Undermining and Enchancing Effects of Reward on Intrinsic Motivation." In *Teacher-Student Perceptions: Implications for Learning.* Edited by J. Levine and M. Wang. Morristown, N.J.: Erlbaum, 1982.

Redl, F. *When We Deal With Children.* New York: Free Press, 1966.

Rist, R. "Student Social Class and Teacher Expectations: The Self-Fulfilling Prophecy of Ghetto Education." *Harvard Educational Review* 40 (1970): 411-451.

Rohrkemper, M. M. "Classroom Perspectives Study: An Investigation of Differential Perceptions of Classroom Events." Doctoral dissertation, Michigan State University, 1981.

Rohrkemper, M. M., and Brophy, J. E. *Classroom Strategy Study: Investigating Teacher Strategies with Problem Students.* Research Series No. 50. East Lansing, Mich.: Institute for Research on Teaching, Michigan State University, 1979.

Rohrkemper, M. M., and Brophy, J. E. *The Influence of Problem Ownership on Teachers' Perceptions of and Strategies for Coping with Problem Students.* Research Series No. 84. East Lansing, Mich.: Institute for Research on Teaching, Michigan State University, 1980a.

Rohrkemper, M. M., and Brophy, J. E. *Teachers' General Strategies for Dealing with Problem Students.* Research Series No. 87. East Lansing, Mich.: Institute for Research on Teaching, Michigan State University, 1980b.

Rohrkemper, M., and Brophy, J. "Teachers' Thinking About Problem Students." In *Teacher-Student Perceptions: Implications for Learning.* Edited by J. Levine and M. Wang. Morristown, N.J.: Erlbaum, 1982.

Rohrkemper, M. M., and Brophy, J. "Student Motivation Study: Interview Protocols." East Lansing, Mich.: Michigan State University, in progress.

Rosenthal, R., and Jacobson, L. *Pygmalion in the Classroom: Teacher Expectation and Pupils' Intellectual Development.* New York: Holt, Rinehart and Winston, 1968.

Ross, M. "The Self-Perception of Intrinsic Motivation." In *New Directions in Attributional Research, Vol. I.* Edited by Harvey, Ickes, and Kidd. New York: Erlbaum, 1976.

Shavelson, R. "Teachers' Decision Making." In *The Psychology of Teaching Methods. The 75th Yearbook of the National Society for the Study of Education, Part I.* Edited by N. Gage. Chicago: University of Chicago Press, 1976.

Simon, H. *The Sciences of the Artificial.* Cambridge, Mass.: MIT Press, 1969.

Stallings, J.; Needels, M.; and Stayrook, N. *How to Change the Process of Teaching Basic Reading Skills in Secondary Schools: Phase II and Phase III.* Menlo Park, Calif.: SRI International, 1979.

Stollak, G.; Scholom, A.; Kallman, J.; and Saturansky, C. "Insensitivity to Children: Responses of Undergraduates to Children in Problem Situations." *Journal of Abnormal Child Psychology* 1 (1973): 169-180.

Walberg, H. "Psychology of Learning Environments: Behavioral, Structural, or Perceptual?" In *Review of Research in Education, Vol. 4.* Edited by L. S. Shulman. New York: Peacock, 1976.

Weiner, B. "A Theory of Motivation for Some Classroom Experiences." *Journal of Educational Psychology* 71 (1979): 3-25.

Weinstein, R. Personal communication, 1980.

Weinstein, R., and Middlestadt, S. "Student Perceptions of Teacher Intentions with Male High and Low Achievers." *Journal of Educational Psychology* 71 (1979): 421-431.

Winne, P., and Marx, R. "Reconceptualizing Research on Teaching." *Journal of Educational Psychology* 69 (1977): 668-678.

Wolf, R. L. *Strategies for Conducting Naturalistic Evaluation in Socio-Educational Settings: The Naturalistic Interview.* Occasional Paper Series. Kalamazoo, Mich.: Evaluation Center, Western Michigan University, 1979.

Yarrow, L. J. "Interviewing Children." In *Handbook of Research Methods in Child Development.* Edited by P. H. Mussen. New York: Wiley and Sons, 1960.

The author wishes to acknowledge and thank Linda Anderson, Jere Brophy, and Rhona Weinstein for their comments on an earlier draft, and June Smith for her assistance in manuscript preparation.

Part Three: Classroom Management in Context

6

School Settings and Their Keeping

Paul V. Gump

W HEN we propose to manage classrooms, what exactly do we intend to manage? While difficult incidents and problem children catch our attention and require our response, these matters amount to a kind of compelling punctuation of a more basic flow of happenings in the classroom.

Fundamentally, the operations of classrooms focus on the settings, or segments, that make up the classroom day. Segments of the classroom environment consist of what we usually call lessons, but they also include opening routines, housekeeping sessions, recreational interludes, and other activities that round out school time.

In this chapter we'll look at the segment structure of classrooms. Different kinds of segments used in the classroom yield different kinds and degrees of pupil involvement, and they require different management techniques. Knowledge of such aspects of classroom functioning should assist teachers in their schoolkeeping efforts.

The Basic Classroom Unit

The classroom is an environment made up of subsections. While it is easy to characterize certain events—such as a whole-class vocabulary lesson or a small-group session on long division—as aspects of curriculum, they are also segments of the classroom environment. Segments show the following basic characteristics (Barker, 1968):

1. *An action structure.* The basic idea of an action structure is illustrated in games. In a game of tag, the actions are chasing and fleeing; the goal of the action is for the "it" to tag, for other players to avoid the tag. Furthermore, the game specifies the sequence of action roles: when "it" chases and tags a player, that player becomes the new "it." This very simple game has an action structure that specifies who shall do what, to whom, when. Well established action structures in school are like games; they prescribe action *goals,* the *actions* themselves, *who* shall engage in

which actions, and *when*. The action structure is the heart of classroom segments.

2. *The physical milieu.* The action structure requires a site and facilities (supplies, tools, furniture, and so on). The physical arrangement is not itself a segment (as the word is used here) but the hull or "container" for the segments.

3. *A fit between the action structure and the milieu.* A teacher may assemble a small group of pupils in a semicircle around a blackboard in the rear of the room. Problems will be put on the board and pupils will learn how to solve them. For this activity to be successful, there must be a fit between the physical milieu and the action structure. That is, the chairs must be placed so that the students are oriented toward the blackboard. The action structure of inspecting the problems requires that the blackboard be high enough to be visible and that line of sight to the board remain unobstructed. The teacher also hopes that the children will be receptive to each other's ideas; the semicircle arrangement (as opposed to a row-and-column set-up) makes face-to-face interaction possible. This is another fit between the action structure (one supposed to involve much inter-pupil communication) and the milieu.

Most physical arrangements are usually not "good" or "bad" in themselves but in terms of their desired fit to the action structure and its purposes. For example, another teacher might decide that pupils should *not* share their misconceptions about long division; this teacher hopes to establish an action structure that calls for attention to the teacher and the blackboard and not to fellow pupils. In this case, the milieu semi-circle arrangement would not fit the desired action structure.

4. *A set of spatial and temporal boundaries.* Classroom segments sometimes use the entire room; at other times they require a reasonably well-bounded segment of that space. Segments also have bounded time spans; a class vocabulary review might begin at 9:16 and end at 9:29.

The Basic Units in Clusters

The units just described, the classroom segments, occur in sequence and sometimes parallel each other throughout the school day. They are encompassing, complete at the environmental level. Events in the classroom occur in one segment or another, or in transitions between them; the students and the teacher are physically located in one or the other of the segments.

An actual cluster of classroom segments as recorded for Mrs. Carr, a third-grade teacher, appears in Figure 1. The morning began at 8:45 with a pre-class "study period" during which students could study or

Figure 1

A Map of Mrs. Carr's Classroom Segments for One Quarter of a Day
(Vertical distances show durations; horizontal distances indicate population size.)

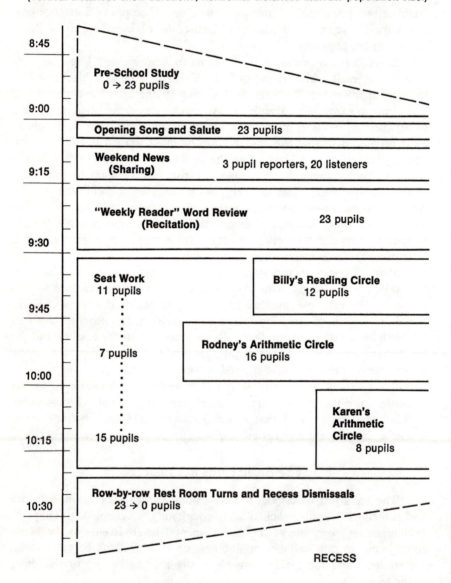

converse quietly. When the buzzer signaled at 9:00, the official period started with singing and the flag salute. This was Monday, so Mrs. Carr encouraged a sharing of "weekend news." After reviewing the vocabulary that would be important in the *Weekly Reader,* at 9:30 the class split into parallel segments labeled seatwork and reading circles. Over time, three separate circle segments operated. Finally, a fairly extended and structured dismissal routine got students out to morning recess.

Four aspects of these segments provide the outline for our consideration of the segment structure and management issues.

1. *Active input vs. passive availability of materials.* The action structures for the word review and the seatwork segments differ along a dimension described as active input versus passive availability of materials and events. In the word review, external events—in this case the teacher's questions, other pupil answers, teacher's response—actively invite pupils' attention and participation. That to which pupils are to attend and the sequencing of this attention is actively "sent" from the situation to the pupil. The events, the input from the segment environment, continuously pace pupil participation. Other examples of active input segments include those in which active displays "call for" participant attention, such as TV lessons, audio tapes, and academic games.

In contrast to the word review action structure, the seatwork action structure uses materials (texts, workbooks, papers, assignment sheets), but these are passive. What to do from moment to moment is not pressed upon pupils; rather, to move forward in the activity students must depend on the clarity and vigor of their own plans. While an assignment sheet may offer overall guidance, the specific moves and their timing depend on the pupils, not active external pacing. Settings other than seatwork can involve the passive availability action structure, such as individual arts or crafts projects, or library searches to develop reports.

The dimension of active input versus passive availability is of fundamental importance when considering issues of pupil involvement and teacher management approaches.

2. *Independent vs. interdependent participants.* Another dimension of action structure implicit in the seatwork and the reading circle is the independence versus the interdependence of participants. In seatwork, students are expected to read their own materials and develop their own answers. Pupils work independent of each other. However, in the reading circle, pupils are expected to attend to one another's contributions, evaluate them, sometimes correct or supplement them. In a well-run recitation, pupils are expected to use others' actions as keys to their own. The action structure requires pupil-pupil interdependence. Pupil-pupil interdependence is even more continuous and demanding in academic

games; participants' actions and counteractions are at the core of game activity.

3. *Single vs. parallel segments.* The characteristics described above apply to individual segments; but some qualities also derive from segments' relationships to one another. One of these relationship qualities is the operation of single versus parallel segments. Note the situation in Figure 1 from 9:30 to 10:20. Most parallel segments provide active input (often a teacher-led recitation) for one segment and passive availability of materials and events for the other. The passive availability action structure is usually presumed to "run itself," thus freeing the teacher for her continuous activity in the parallel active input segment. If the teachers' efforts are required in the passive availability segment, the double or overlapping requirements pose a managerial problem.

4. *Transitions.* Obvious parts of the segment structure displayed in Figure 1 are the breaks occurring between segments. During these transitions, persons, materials, places, and mental sets must change. Successful management of transitions is important in guiding the classroom day.

We can turn now to consideration of each of the four issues just described and note what research has established regarding the nature of the segment structure involved and the implications for classroom management.

Action Structures with Active Input vs. Passive Availability

Investigations have shown that pupil involvement can be related to whether the action structures of the segments call for active input of stimuli or merely passive availability of materials and events. In a study of third grades, the average pupil involvement scores in all active input segments was 85 percent, and 75 percent in passive availability segments (Gump, 1967). Another study involving grades one through five showed pupil involvement in the recitation segments (active input) to be 85 percent, yet only 65 percent in the seatwork (passive availability) segments. Deviancy (misconduct beyond simple noninvolved behavior) was almost four times as frequent in the seatwork segments (Kounin and others, 1966).

During seatwork the teacher often attends to another segment while the seatwork pupils are without immediate supervision. We might assume that the teacher's presence causes pupils to be more involved in active input segments. However, when teachers monitored seatwork (without substantial input), pupil involvement scores in passive input segments were much lower than in active input segments; scores, in fact, were the same as when the teacher was busy elsewhere in the room.

Active input segments, as they most often occur in elementary schools, result in less misbehavior and more involvement than passive availability segments.

One exception to the general success of active input segments deserves attention because it sharpens our understanding of how the segment structure can affect pupil behavior. As we reflect on the matter, it seems clear that active input segments usually result in more continuous pupil involvement because of the "pull" that external signals provide. Professionals (teachers or those who construct film strips, movies, and so forth) know how to keep the signals for action clear, on-target, and forward moving. However, it is quite possible for major signal givers in active input segments to be nonprofessional. They may even be children: report givers, sharers, discussers. Children may not be the most adequate presenters, however. They falter; repeat themselves; omit important information; and provide less adequate, less forward-moving input than do professional presenters. Using children as major signal givers can lead to relatively low pupil involvement in active input segments. The third-grade segments in which students were the major signal givers showed the lowest pupil involvement rate of all segment types observed. Active input segments continuously led by the teacher resulted in 87 percent involvement rates, but segments with prolonged student contributions (sharing, reporting, student-student discussion) showed only 72 percent (Gump, 1967). Later research from nusery school segments verified less overall involvement in active input segments that depended heavily on student contribution. In this study, active input segments in which the teacher was the primary signal giver (teacher reads story, teacher makes demonstration) resulted in high involvement. Segments with much student discussion ("Let's all tell what jobs our parents have") gave significantly reduced pupil involvement.

Management of Active Input Segments

The pupil response to active input segments has been presented so far in terms of whatever management may have prevailed. However, certain teacher behaviors can increase or decrease pupil involvement in these kinds of segments.

One set of beneficial teacher behaviors (Kounin, 1970) is labeled Group Alerting. For example, the teacher may say with some challenge: "Let's all think about this; it may fool you." The teacher may create some suspense about who will be asked to contribute. Group Alerting was significantly associated with increased pupil involvement and decreased pupil deviancy (r's $= .60$ and $.44$).

Other teacher actions improving pupil involvement in the active input segments were those maintaining forward movement, the momentum of the action structure. In other words, the teacher avoided what Kounin called "slowdowns." These interruptions to momentum could include mini-lectures on misbehavior, overtalking about how certain actions must be carried out, or how tools and materials are to be handled. Absence of slowdowns was related to increased involvement and decreased deviance in the active input segments (r's = .66 and .64).

The tendency for action structures with major dependence on student presenters to yield lower involvement scores is related to this issue of momentum. Probably pupil presentation, in many cases, slows down the forward flow of the active input segments and nonpresenting pupils lose interest. One method of counteracting this loss of momentum is to limit pupil presentation. Kounin and Sherman (1979) showed that when teachers keep pupil contributions short, overall pupil involvement improves. Fortunately, it is *not* a matter of less total pupil participation; it requires that the individual contributions not be extended. Other data from the elementary school indicate that teacher "immersion in one reciter" produces lower group involvement. These findings certainly do not prove that extended pupil contributions should always be avoided; the teacher may decide they are valuable enough to accept the temporary cost in lowered pupil involvement. It is realistic to be aware of the cost, however.

It is clear that for active input segments, the issue of momentum in the external environment is a very important factor. With momentum, latent tendencies to inattention and possible misbehavior are often swept aside; without forward-moving external events, these tendencies become overt and proliferate.

Management of Passive Availability Segments

The most typical passive segments are those labeled seatwork. The action structures for these segments call for self-pacing; since external signals are not going to prod participant action, internal signals and those derived from interaction with passive external objects and events must be sufficient. Obviously, preparation has both a cognitive and a motivational aspect. That is, students need to know what to do and be interested in doing it. On the cognitive side, the teacher can help preparation by explaining, rehearsing sample tasks, writing lists of steps to be taken, and so on. On the motivational side, Kounin (1970) found that pupil involvement increases when teachers indicate that something about the activity is fun or interesting; or when they challenge the participants: "Some of these are not as easy as they look; I wonder how many of them you can actually do."

After even adequate preparation, the internal signals that sustain seatwork activity over time can lose vigor. This seems especially true when one has had relief from this sedentary activity and then must return to it. In one study, pupil involvement in seatwork was especially low after a return from recess (Gump, 1967). One method to eliminate this period of low motivation is for the teacher to deal with seatwork people first after recess (rather than starting the parallel reading circle segment). The teachers asked children about their progress and answered questions about how to proceed. Only after ensuring that seatwork children were "back on track" did the teachers begin the parallel small-group activity.

Probably the most pervasive problem in seatwork is boredom; Kounin has characterized the disinclination to continue repetitive activity as *satiation*. Research on repetitive activity shows satiation effects in two directions: the activity becomes less attractive over time, and changes occur in task behavior (often deteriorations). Kounin reasoned that if satiation operated in seatwork sessions, decreasing the degree of repetitions—or, in positive terms—increasing the amount of action structure variety should increase pupil involvement.

Teachers' efforts to increase variety in classroom activity are different than the management behaviors discussed thus far. Variety within the segment structure is created more by *arrangements* of program and materials than by communications to pupils. For example, the teacher may schedule the span of seatwork activity such that pupils change the subject matter with which they deal; the teacher may see to it that the primary objects being used are shifted (pupils compute first with pencil and paper, then with an abacus); the task behavior may be shifted from, for example, "reading about the voyage" to drawing several pictures to depict the voyage. Finally, tasks with intellectual challenge (solving anagrams) create more variety than tasks that require only concentration and repetition (writing each spelling word three times).

In two different studies, Kounin looked for a significant relationship between the amount of variety the teacher builds into a classroom segment and the amount of pupil involvement.

Variety had *no* relationship to pupil involvement in the teacher-led segments (in our terms, in the active input action structures); however, there was a substantial relation between these variables in the seatwork or passive availabiliy segments. Children in first and second grades in high variety segments were much more involved than children in low variety segments. This result, which held for two investigations, illustrates the principle that the efficacy of teacher strategies is highly dependent on the kind of segment operating.

For one study, children in grades three to five were *not* helped by variety. (Older children were not subjects in the second investigations.)

This surprising result might mean that the amount of variety that is most effective depends on the maturity of the child. Kounin speculated that the older youngsters required more sense of "felt progress," and frequent changes of activity interfered with this experience.

Before leaving the consideration of the passive availability segments and their management, it might be instructive to look at such segments when they received generally high involvement.

In a nursery school study, Kounin and Gump (1974) analyzed 596 lessons in terms of their program dimensions and pupil behavior. The lesson group that obtained the highest involvement of the six types investigated was one involving *individual construction* (specifically, each child made his or her own valentine). In this action structure, the child had no active external input; the child developed moves from interaction with essentially passive materials. While one might explain high involvement with the observation that "children like to make things," this did not seem satisfactory. Children liked most of their nursery school lessons. Furthermore, when engaged in *group* projects of construction (making a mural together), involvement was significantly lower.

What happened in the individual construction activity to account for the unusually high pupil involvement? Description of another segment may help. Students are given materials for making a face with a paper pie plate—the plate; colored bits of paper for the eyes, nose, mouth; and paste and scissors. As the child begins his project, he may paste on a blue piece for an eye, which suggests the need for the second eye which is quickly attached. Now it becomes obvious that the object "calls for" a nose—then a mouth, perhaps ears, or hair as well. In this structure, there is a tight circle of action; the child physically creates a changed situation that suggests another action leading to more completeness but also to further incompleteness, and so on. An individual—immersed in an action/feedback-from-action/further action cycle—is insulated against distraction and capable of relatively intensive and persistent concentration and involvement.

This involvement is demonstrated in cases where misbehavior occurs. In other kinds of nursery school action structures, deviancy by one child is likely to be contagious; it can trigger deviancy in others. Such contagion was very rare in the individual construction activity (Davenport, 1976).

Even individual construction lessons taught by the same teachers varied in degree of pupil involvement. Lowered involvement could occur when required materials were unavailable ("Where's the paste?") or ineffective ("These scissors won't cut the cardboard"). Involvement could also be lowered if the child's action did not result in "what's next" feedback. (If one is to make an abstract design, how does one know what comes next?

Or when one is finished?) Teachers may need to make sure materials are available and clarify possible steps in some construction action structures.

Discussion to this point has centered on the action structure dimension of active input versus passive availability of materials and events. We can also consider how the action structure specifies participant interaction. For example, certain segments involve pupils providing the input for one another. A basic difference among action structures can be the extent to which they require participants to interlock their actions. The interdependence of pupil actions is clear in academic games, in discussions, and in "team projects." Action structures that require strong interdependency often influence how participants come to regard one another.

Action Structures with Interdependence of Pupil Participants

An example of an action structure with high pupil-pupil interdependency is provided by Aronson's "jig saw" format (Aronson and others, 1978). Students are divided into small groups. At the first small-group meeting each child is assigned a section of the lesson, and the responsibility for teaching that section to other children in the group. If the lesson involved the life of a famous person, for example, one pupil might be asked to teach about that person's childhood, another his early adulthood, and so on.

Each child in the group then goes to a "counterpart" group—one composed of those children with the same assignment as his own. In this small group, all work together deciding on how to present material, how to answer anticipated questions, and so on. After helping one another prepare, the children return to their original group to teach. As each child offers his or her section, the lesson is put together as a "jigsaw." Important in this operation is the essentiality of each person. Grades for group members depend on mastery of the entire lesson. Pupils are thus pressed to encourage, and to listen to, one another. The jigsaw method has resulted in a number of improvements in interpersonal relationships—less need to "beat classmates at school work," more liking for and being liked by other students.

The jigsaw technique was devised to yield better social integration of minority groups; research has shown improved integration (Aronson and others, 1978). As an added bonus, children in the jigsaw arrangement reported they were less bored by school and liked it more. The jig saw arrangement is one of a number of interdependency formats researchers have employed. (An interested reader might want to check recent reviews by Gump, 1980; Sharan, 1980; Slavin, 1980.) Furthermore, certain conditions—cooperative, as opposed to competitive or individualistic action structures—can yield improved subject matter learning (see a review by Johnson and others, 1981).

The importance of activity structure in affecting not only pupil-pupil social relationships but pupil-teacher relationships has been documented by Bossert (1979). Teachers may sense that negative interpersonal relationships may be involved in classroom problems. They may exhort children to "be more cooperative." Using the interdependency formats, teachers can work at a more primary level, putting children into action structures that require extensive cooperative actions, which develop more general cooperative attitudes and behaviors.

Parallel Segments and Overlapping Situations

Referring back to Figure 1, during the 9:30 to 10:20 period, two segments functioned simultaneously: Seatwork and Billy's Reading Circle, Seatwork and Rodney's Arithmetic Circle, and Seatwork and Karen's Arithmetic Circle. Continuous teacher actions were required to manage the reading and arithmetic circles: we can label these teacher-initiative segments. The seatwork action structure, a pupil-initiative segment, was presumed to require little or no teacher contribution once it was under way. Teachers often establish such parallel segments so they can deal directly with small groups; here frequent and close pupil-pupil and teacher-pupil interaction is more feasible than it is in total class assemblies.

The vulnerability of the parallel segment arrangement is the possibility that teachers will be called on to deal with events in the pupil-initiative segment. When teachers are pressed to act in two different segments at the same time, they are placed in one type of overlapping situation. The managerial problem here is challenging. Not only must teachers process information from two sources, but they are urged to act in two directions. Acting appropriately toward one situation can conflict with acting adequately toward the other. A common classroom example occurs when the teacher investigates and then settles the "trouble" in seatwork but has to withdraw her necessary input to the reading circle in the process. Since the reading circle action depends on continuous teacher action, the withdrawal of that action can lead to much loss of pupil involvement.

In order to appreciate the overlapping problem, we can review data for a 78-minute span of parallel segments managed by a beginning teacher. Although we might expect almost all teacher action in this period to be directed to the teacher-initiative circles, a total of 96 actions were addressed to the parallel pupil-initiative segments. As a result, pupil involvement in the circles dropped sharply; the progress the teacher had planned for the material was not accomplished, an outcome the teacher regretted: "We didn't seem to get too far today."

What generated the many calls for teacher attention to the segments that were supposed to operate on pupil initiative? Analysis of the teacher actions showed that 40 percent were behavior facilitative (trying to help students who had problems with process or with tools and supplies, and giving recognition for work accomplished). Observation of the pupil behavior in the seatwork segment showed that a number of children could not handle the assigned art project. Teacher help, in the children's view, was required. Clearly, either a less complex and novel task needed to be assigned, or some kind of "walk-through" practice with the teacher was necessary before pupils began the seatwork.

Another teacher behavior also generated calls from the seatwork group. When one student finished a bit of artwork, she left the seatwork and approached the teacher for comment. The teacher offered pleasant recognition. Unfortunately this event, watched carefully by other seatwork children, resulted in others coming by ones and twos to the teacher to have their efforts recognized. Finally, the teacher had to ask that this sharing of work wait until the end of the circle activity.

Clearly, the teacher was attempting to "meet the needs of the children" with these behavior facilitative actions. However, this effort for the seatwork children caused her to fail to meet the needs of the circle children to experience a forward-moving and complete lesson.

Fifty percent of the teacher attentions to the seatwork group were behavior corrective. "Why are you not at your seat?" "Attend to your work and not to Mary." It is highly likely that the off-task behavior resulted to some extent from the difficulty of the task. But a number of corrections may not have been necessary. The teacher was oriented toward doing something about each minor deviancy immediately; at times her intervention distracted the students more than the deviancy. Work in both segments often stopped as pupils checked out the event. Not all deviancy is best handled as it occurs; the distraction cost may be too great. For those that must be handled, the teacher needs to be less intrusive, possibly by using silent signals or physical moves toward the seatwork problem while maintaining input to the circle group.

The handling of overlapping situations was investigated by Kounin (1970). In classes where teachers were able to deal with both situations without becoming immersed in one situation to the exclusion of the other, pupils were more involved in teacher-initiative segments and less deviant in pupil-initiative segments.

In general, effective approaches to overlapping situations require attention to the generation of overlapping situations as well as to the method of handling them once they occur. When more than one segment operates, it is important to establish a pupil-initiative segment that pupils can manage. Furthermore, it is usually better not to invite overlapping by rewarding children's intrusions from the pupil initiative segment. When overlapping must be dealt with, it is clear that short, nonobtrusive approaches disturb the classroom business least.

Transitions and Options for Their Management

In principle, there are three phases of transitions between one segment and another: the closeout of the first segment, some kind of "moving over" (physical or psychological), and an entering into the second segment. Transitions always involve a change in the segment concern or "business" and in the orientations of the teacher and students. They may also require changes in objects, physical location, behavior mode (from writing to listening), and personnel.

When transitions do not go well, they can consume much educational time. In one study of open-space and traditional schools, the overall amount of time that was *not* invested in educational activity amounted to 21 percent (Gump, 1974). Most of this noneducational time went into transitions. And when the programs of the schools involved frequent changes of site, the noneducational time rose to 27 percent. On an afternoon in late spring when teachers in one open school seemed to relax the transition management, the noneducational time reached 40 percent.

The fact that transitions can create managerial problems is suggested by changes in teacher behavior. In a study of six third-grade teachers for two days, each teacher on both days increased her behavior-corrective activity for transitions. Although the amount varied markedly between teachers, each teacher increased behavior corrections at transitions (Gump, 1969). Other data show that teachers deal with children on a one-to-one basis much more frequently during transitions between segments than during the segments themselves.

One reason the teacher behaves differently at transitions is that the children change their behavior. In a study of 50 classes managed by student teachers, Arlin (1979) found that off-task behavior in transitions was almost double the rate occurring in nontransition activities. The data were consistent over five different sets of schools studied.

What is involved in the problems that accompany transitions? First, there may be problems in removing students from the interests and actions of the first segment. Arlin noted that if students come from a physically stimulating segment, such as recess or gym, into a more sedentary segment, much off-task behavior may result.

A second transition problem involves losing the structure that deterred deviancy and off-task behavior during the first segment. Without a second structure, children are likely to do what comes naturally.

A third factor is that students have "saved up" problems or tensions during the first segment and deal with them during the more open transition period. (Children seem to wait for the opportunity to ask something, show something, move about, talk to their neighbor, and so on.) Saving up requests to the teacher is often a part of the classroom rule system established to free the teacher from interruptions during times when he or she must actively lead a subgroup. Extensions of transition periods for this purpose are probably legitimate; however, the possible loss of activity momentum is a consideration.

A fourth transition problem may arise in the beginning of the second segment if there are delays. Entering into the action of the second segment is often frustrated by delays. The teacher may be dealing with individual children or assembling materials. In some cases, the teacher is held up because she is still involved with another group. Delay in *starting* the second segment is much more often responsible for excessive transition time than is the time required to move pupils and materials *to* the second segment.

There are two solutions to these problems. For example, children may need some help in detaching themselves from the first segment; obviously the more interested they are, the more they need a kind of advance warning and a "wrap up" to move away from the first segment and into the next. For some problems, the second segment needs a different introduction. When Krantz and Risley (1977) found that going from recess directly to story time produced 37 percent off-task behavior in the beginning of story time, they inserted a "rest period" before the story and reduced off-task behavior to 14 percent.

Not all transitions must involve a temporary loss of the action structures that guide behavior. Although Arlin (1979) found that transitions, overall, yielded much higher off-task behaviors than other periods, he established an important second finding. He examined a subgroup of student teachers who managed both structured and unstructured transitions. (In structured transitions procedures of transition were present: a statement of how soon the first segment must end, some kind of wrap-up of the first segment, a procedure or routine for managing objects or moving across space, and so forth.) Arlin discovered that structured transitions yielded significantly less disruption than unstructured ones; in fact, there was *no* significant difference in off-task behavior between *structured* transitions and nontransitional periods.

The structured transition maintains a behavior-guiding action system;

the momentum of activity is preserved.

Kounin (1977) described several negative teacher behaviors at transition that related to momentum. He called these behaviors "dangle" and "flip-flop." When a teacher starts a transition and then gets caught up in another matter and leaves that line of action, the students are left to "dangle" until she returns. A "flip-flop" occurs when the teacher terminates one activity, begins another, then returns to the matters of the first activity. Kounin showed that such teacher behaviors were associated with less on-task behavior. He did not test their effects on the transition period itself; however, they manifestly interfere with forward movement in transition periods.

Attention must be given to getting a good start after a transition. Jones and Jones (1981) list a number of pointers for the beginning of an activity. These authors, as well as Arlin (1979), emphasize the importance of having everyone's attention before beginning. When information is to be given that everyone must have, this advice may be accurate. However, the ideas about momentum apply as well. A major force pulling children into an active input segment is that "something is happening." A teacher who can get such segments under way will often draw the nonattending children in; waiting for absolute and universal attention can sometimes lead to unnecessarily extended transition times.

In the long run, pointers for handling transitions will prove less useful than a basic understanding of what is really happening during these changes of action and at what phase of the change. Elaborate structures and rules for transitions, although orderly, can take up an inordinate amount of the children's time. Prescott (1973) found that in well-structured day care facilities 26 percent of the children's time was occupied in transitions. Less structured day care arrangements consumed less of the children's existence in the secondary process of getting from one activity to another.

Reflections

When we think of managing classrooms, we need a starting place. That place, as described here, is the organization of the classroom's mini-environments or segments. The segments are tangible "out there" sections of environment and function as contexts for more particular aspects of teacher and pupil action.

The segment consists of a bounded action structure that is anchored to a physical milieu (facilities, supplies, and so forth). While this discussion has not emphasized the physical aspects of the classroom, a complete description of segment organization would have detailed their influence. Studies by Weinstein (1981) and Smith and Connally (1980) show the relationships between such matters as amount of space, seating arrangements, or kind and amount of physical resources, to pupil behavior.

The use of a segment framework provides a structured vision of a classroom in operation. Crucial aspects of this operation can be systematically considered, perhaps manipulated. The knowledge that a particular segment's action structure depends on active teacher inputs suggests that pupil involvement may be relatively continuous, but only as long as the teacher's input is also reasonably continuous. The knowledge that a segment's arrangements can call for cooperative, competitive, or individualistic actions among pupils provides opportunity for changing social interaction patterns and, over time, actual social relationships. Sensitivity to the opportunities and vulnerabilities of simultaneous segments should make management of classroom affairs more adequate. Understanding what facilitates and what retards transitions between segments can help maintain classroom momentum and avoid loss of valuable educational time.

This chapter first stressed the qualities of segment structure and only later examined teacher behavior. This ordering was deliberate. While teacher behavior is obviously crucial in determining the success of classroom operations, its importance is relative to two aspects of the segment framework. The teacher's behavior *is* important in terms of the segment structure he or she decides to establish. To this extent, the structure is subservient to teachers' decisions. However, once the structure is established, the behavior of the teacher is coerced by the structure probably more inexorably than is pupil behavior. (Certainly a teacher's failure to behave in ways appropriate to the segment structure will create more widespread and immediate negative effects than a student's temporary failure to attend to his or her studies.) The fact that teacher behavior must be appropriate, even subservient, to the established segment structure has implications for changing and improving teacher behavior. Improvement may depend more on the selection or reform of the segment structure than on new behavior in established segment arrangements. For example, if teachers rely mostly on total-class, teacher-initiative segments, it will be difficult for them to deal personally and at length with any one student. Attempts to create this sort of "interpersonal warmth" will be more congenial to small groups in which pupil initiative is a part of the action structure.

Much of the research cited here has compared effects of established segment structure. However, the material dealing with interdependent action structures ("jigsaw," for instance) involved creation of new action structures to obtain desired social outcomes. Other teacher goals could generate manipulation of segments. To awaken learners, one might devise highly focused and rapidly moving active input segments; to balance this pressing approach, one might give students much choice in segments involving passive availability of materials and events. Such efforts depend on the creativity of individual teachers. A segment framework with its research base provides a beginning theory for segment manipulation.

References

Arlin, M. "Teacher Transitions Can Disrupt Time Flow in Classrooms." *American Educational Research Journal* 16 (1979): 42-56.

Aronson, E.; Bridgeman, D. L.; and Geffner, R. "The Effects of a Cooperative Classroom Structure on Student Behavior and Attitudes." In *Social Psychology of Education*. Edited by D. Bar-Tal and L. Saxe. New York: Halsted, 1978.

Bossert, S. T. *Tasks and Social Relationships in Classrooms*. New York: Cambridge Press, 1979.

Barker, R. G. *Ecological Psychology*. Stanford, Calif.: Stanford University Press, 1968.

Davenport, G. G. "The Effects of Lessons Signals System Upon the Duration and Spread of Deviancy." Doctoral dissertation, Wayne State University, 1976.

Gump, P. V. "The Classroom Behavior Setting: Its Nature and Relation to Student Behavior." U.S. Office of Education Cooperative Research Branch, Project #5-0334, Final Report, 1967. (Mimeographed.)

Gump, P. V. "Intra-Setting Analysis: The Third Grade Classroom as a Special But Instructive Case." In *Naturalistic Viewpoints in Psychological Research*. Edited by E. Williams and H. Raush. New York: Holt, Rinehart and Winston, 1969.

Gump, P. V. "The School as a Social Situation." *Annual Review of Psychology* 31 (1980): 553-582.

Johnson, D. W.; Maruyama, G.; Johnson, R.; Nelson, D.; and Skon, L. "Effects of Cooperative, Competitive and Individualistic Goal Structures on Achievement: A Meta-Analysis." *Psychological Bulletin* 89 (1981): 47-62.

Jones, V. F., and Jones, L. S. *Responsible Classroom Discipline*. Boston: Allyn and Bacon, 1981.

Kounin, J. S. *Discipline and Group Management in Classrooms*. New York: Holt, Rinehart and Winston, 1970.

Kounin, J. S.; Freisen, W.; and Norton, A. E. "Managing Emotionally Disturbed Children in Regular Classrooms." *Journal of Educational Psychology* 57 (1966): 1-3.

Kounin, J. S., and Gump, P. V. "Signal Systems of Lesson Settings and the Task-Related Behavior of Pre-School Children." *Journal of Educational Research* 66 (1977): 554-562.

Kounin, J. S., and Sherman, L. W. "School Environments as Behavior Settings." *Theory Into Practice* 13 (1979): 145-151.

Krantz, P. J., and Risley, T. R. "Behavioral Ecology in the Classroom." In *Classroom Management: The Successful Use of Behavior Modification*. 2nd ed. Edited by K. D. O'Leary and S. G. O'Leary. New York: Pergamon Press, 1977.

Prescott, E. "Who Thrives in Day Care?" Pasadena, Calif.: Pacific Oaks College, 1973. (Mimeographed.)

Sharan, S. "Cooperative Learning in Small Groups: Recent Methods and Effects on Achievement, Attitudes and Ethnic Relations." *Review of Educational Research* 50 (1980): 241-271.

Slavin, R. E. "Cooperative Learning." *Review of Educational Research* 50 (1980): 315-342.

Smith, P. K., and Connally, K. S. *The Ecology of Preschool Behaviour*. New York: Cambridge University Press, 1980.

Weinstein, C. S. "Classroom Design as an External Condition for Learning." *Educational Technology* 21 (1981): 12-19.

7

Creating a Living Curriculum for Teaching Self-Discipline

William W. Wayson and Gay Su Pinnell

M OST approaches to school discipline focus on the wrong things. They do little to alleviate problems and often produce the very behavior they are designed to end. The basic problem is that because we start from wrong conceptions about what causes "undisciplined" behavior, we thus do the wrong things with the best of intentions.

Among a small proportion of students, "bad" behavior is traceable to some chemical dysfunction, some quirk in the chromosomes, or some defect in previous experience that has resulted in a mental disorder. Such students are relatively rare, certainly rarer by far than the folklore of schools would have us believe. Most behavior (and misbehavior is behavior) is caused by the objects and the events in the world around the student and the particular way in which the student relates to that world. We cannot understand the behavior without understanding both the world around the student and the peculiarly personal way in which the student selects parts of that world and reacts to them. We also have to understand that the peculiarly personal way of relating is *learned*. The objects and events that surround the student as powerfully, as fully, and for so long a period of time as they do in a school constantly *teach* the student how to react to the school, just as churches or theaters contain forces that *teach* us how to behave in their confines.[1] We need to know also that it is much easier and more productive to alter the world around students than it is to change students' psychological makeup or to directly affect the way they have come to react to the world. Furthermore, as educators, we can much more easily affect the environment in which students learn how to behave at school than we can the home or community environment.

---

[1] We are indebted to Kurt Lewin (1951) and his students and followers for adding so much to our understanding of the relationship between human behavior and the world as the person experiences it. See also Combs (1962).

The Nature of Discipline

In the interest of attaining some mutual agreement and understanding before we proceed, let's use as an example a person walking in the woods. There are literally millions of objects around (if we count leaves and pebbles). Yet when a snake crawls onto the path, all else disappears from vision or knowing and the snake seems to be all that is in the world at the moment. The hapless hiker freezes, jumps, or screams. He *behaves* very peculiarly, but in accordance with how he has learned to behave toward snakes. Of course, another hiker who has learned other behaviors will not relate to the snake in the same way. We might say that the snake caused the first hiker's jumping around. We could say that the hiker was the cause, but even then, we would have to say that some earlier experience with snakes—or someone who was present during experiences with snakes, or the people who produce horror movies or play upon the fear of snakes—has caused the hiker to see snakes the way he does. The *cause* for the behavior may be as much outside the hiker as within.

More to the point of how to teach children to behave in a disciplined manner, we have to admit the wisdom of trying to change the behavior in the presence of snakes by doing something *outside* the learner, rather than trying to attack the learner's behavior or the way he sees snakes. Punishing or belittling the hiker or banishing him from the woods will do little to change his behavior in the presence of snakes, nor will it teach him a better view of snakes. We can be more effective by altering the world around the hiker, by making snakes seem less fearsome, by modeling less fearful behavior, by introducing something that helps him see the snake in more realistic and more productive ways. That way the hiker may behave more productively when we are not around but the snake is.

Disciplinary methods based on the assumption that the student alone is the cause of poor behavior are doomed. They futilely attempt to eliminate symptomatic behaviors that are responses to events going on around the individual. If such events are not changed, they will evoke some form of undesirable response even if we are successful in eliminating the immediate symptom. Our hiker, punished severely for jumping from the snake and screaming, may stop those behaviors but he will wet his pants, get ulcers, hate the one who punishes him, have nightmares, kill other small serpents, or behave in some other way that has little value for himself or for society.

That is precisely what we do in the name of discipline in many schools. That is precisely why poor discipline continues decade after decade to be a major problem in schools and why the same disruptive behaviors occur time and again. That is also why discipline seems to be worsening. Traditionally we have attacked the individual and the symptomatic behavior while the causes in the school around the student have worsened.[2] It is as though we have punished students for shivering while the caulking fell away from the windows, the door warped, and the furnace rusted into disuse. That example may seem extreme, but it is no more far-fetched than suspending students for truancy or punishing a student for misbehaving during her third study hall in one day.

We have not decided what disciplined behavior we want, either. We have viewed discipline only as an undesirable intrusion on the curriculum. We fail to see that self-discipline is the most essential goal of a curriculum that aims to help citizens attain and preserve freedom. Because we do not see that discipline is the heart of a curriculum, we fail to use methods that will stand some chance of teaching the discipline necessary for people in free societies.

Discipline is the ability and the will to do what needs doing for as long as it needs doing and to learn from the results. To truly teach self-discipline and to hold ourselves accountable for it, we must look at factors outside the student. We must see that most of the behavior students exhibit in school is learned in school, just as the behavior they exhibit elsewhere is learned elsewhere. We must find ways to improve practices, habits, structures, and relationships in the school that have a strong influence on the way students see the school, themselves, their peers, the teachers, and the lessons. We can use those changes to teach more productive ways of seeing and relating.

When discipline problems occur in school, they can more often be traced to dysfunctions in the interpersonal climate and organizational patterns of the school than to malfunctions in the individual. In short, misbehaving students are often reacting in a predictable and even sensible way to the school as it affects them and as they have learned to perceive it and react to it. We are not blaming the teacher, the principal, or the custodian for student misbehavior. But we would have them see that the system of roles and relationships in which they engage are often to blame for misbehavior. In most cases, better behavior may be taught more easily by altering patterns of roles and relationships in the school organization than by viewing and treating the student as a pathological problem.

We will not get very far if we continue to manipulate only the superficial characteristics of organizations. For example, school size, the

---

[2] We do not want to join those who exaggerate the problem beyond its actual levels. The fact is that discipline is not as bad in most schools as polls, public opinion, and political opportunists would have us believe. Fifty thousand Frenchmen can be wrong, particularly if they agree that tomatoes are poisonous.

environment. Traditional administrative practice suggests that while teachers make decisions with regard to their own classrooms (and noncertified personnel may make decisions regarding their own duties), they have no responsibility for decisions that affect the overall school organization—hallways, visitors, scheduling, room assignments, and so on. Staff members typically pay little attention to, or feel any responsibility for, the overall operation of the school and for creating an educational environment in areas outside the classroom. Cafeterias, school yards, and hallways are "no man's lands" in which the basic curriculum is left, by default, to the peer culture.

Practices that foster good communication and effective patterns of school decision making and problem solving include:

- Consistently expecting staff members to solve their own problems.

- Teaching staff members the skills they need to solve problems; then letting them use those skills.

- Insisting that anyone who has a problem with anyone else talk with that person about the problem. The supervisory function would be to help individuals learn the skills they need to feel confident enough to make contact.

Objective 2: To reduce authority and status differences.

Authority and status differences often divide people from one another and hamper their participation and sense of responsibility. Smaller status differences and wider participation by the total staff are related to a more responsive system, more widespread sense of responsibility, and greater commitment among staff and students to meet duties and carry out decisions. If a school is to become an organization in which self-discipline is prized and taught, all segments of the staff must be involved.

Staff members must be part of a professional team that includes not only teachers and counselors, but food service workers, aides, security personnel, custodians, school clerks, and others. Only responsible participation by a wide distribution of the whole staff can create the total school climate that is needed to teach discipline most effectively. If staff members do not feel part of the team, individuals and subgroups will work against each other. While responsibilities and individual contributions should be respected, persons in the school should not be fearful and possessive. People have to stop saying, "It's not my job"; territoriality must decrease.

For example, making the cafeteria a more orderly and pleasant place depends on conceiving a plan supported and implemented by a cadre of teachers, food service personnel, and others. Creating a friendly and welcoming atmosphere in the school cannot be accomplished without involving the office staff. Reducing litter and vandalism is much easier if school personnel recognize the important role custodians play in making the school a clean and pleasant place.

Common practices in the school organization reduce participation by emphasizing or creating authority and status differences. Supervisors and specialists often take on specific duties or become possessive of their territory and remove responsibility from classroom teachers. When special reading teachers are available to take classes of students and have little contact with staff, it is easy for staff members to feel that helping students to read is "not their job." When security personnel are employed to give extra supervision in the school, staff members often give up all responsibility for hallway supervision. Social workers and visiting teachers have taken away much of teachers' contact with parents, a contact that gives teachers much status and teaching strength. Having aides for playground supervision is convenient but it tends to deprive teachers of the chance to interact with students in informal ways that could give the teachers much greater influence over the students' behavior and learning. There are many creative ways to provide the free time teachers need for preparation and planning while at the same time allowing for informal interaction with students.

Many central office practices reinforce unnecessary divisions and status levels in the school. Everything from reporting school marks to holding meetings (even the way we address letters or print a directory) will sharpen grade level and departmental distinctions *even when it is not necessary to do so.* Central office politics often prevents sharing resources or cooperating to solve problems. The structure of supervisory and administrative jobs themselves reinforces inferior and superior distinctions that are not useful. Titles on doors and stationery and the priggish use of degrees all heighten class distinctions among school personnel and undermine commitment, responsibility, and self-discipline. If a school staff is paying attention to this factor:

- All staff members feel responsible for the operation of the school.

- People are on a first-name basis throughout all roles.

- Noncertified personnel participate in faculty meetings and inservice sessions.[3]

---

[3] It is, of course, not necessary to have *all* personnel at *all* meetings. Small task forces with representative membership may work on particular problems; departments may need to meet on instructional matters, and so forth. However, activities that affect the whole school are most effectively implemented when staff involvement and responsibilities cut across such divisions.

- All persons in the school are seen as "teachers" with specific responsibilities for teaching students.
- Students observe friendliness and respect among staff members regardless of their roles or departments.
- Important decision groups "cut across" traditional boundaries such as grade levels and departments.
- Students are not divided into low and high status categories.
- Students show respect for all members of the school staff.
- Groups make a conscious effort to communicate with other groups and avoid "segregating" grade levels or other groupings in the lounge and eating areas.
- School social events include all staff members.
- People who ordinarily occupy low status positions do not have to engage in disruptive behavior to protect their egos.

Supervisors and administrators can foster positive relationships in the school by communicating the expectation that all members of the school staff have important roles related to the education of students. Staff meetings and inservice sessions, particularly those focusing on solving the problems of the school, should include noncertified as well as certified personnel. Action plans should specify key activities to be carried out by noncertified personnel.

Some staff development activities should be specifically directed toward building teamwork among the total staff. An activity we have found to be particularly successful in breaking down barriers is an outdoor camping experience similar to Outward Bound.[4] Participants sleep in tents, cook their own food, and complete initiatives such as rappelling down cliffs and getting a group over a 14-foot wall. Those experiences allow personnel to get outside their school roles, see each other as people, and achieve better communication. Not all activities have to be so esoteric; a weekend get-together off school property can really help a school staff work in unison. A local business might provide some retreat facilities. Schmuck and Runkel (1977) describe many ways to improve teamwork and problem solving with school staffs.

Other staff development experiences are not so exotic. Assign important coordinating tasks to people at every level of the organization. Encourage people to try their wings. Consciously break some traditional barriers and help others do the same. For example, a committee of teachers and other staff could set up agendas and run all faculty meetings. Students could conduct most assemblies. Staffs could make more decisions

---

[4] For details, contact the Institute for Creative Living, 363 Fairmont Boulevard, Cleveland, Ohio 44118.

about the budget, class lists, space, resource allocations, and job descriptions than they usually do. Learning how to do new tasks is an excellent motivation for participating in staff development, *and* it elevates staff development—and staff members—to a respected position in the school district.

Some school administrators and supervisors object to these suggestions on grounds that "teachers unions won't let us do that." We have worked in several strong union cities and have had full participation from union staff members to do what is suggested in this chapter. Undoubtedly, there are individual staff members—both union and nonunion—who will not participate in any school, but our experience indicates that blaming the unions has become a self-fulfilling (and sometimes self-protective) prophecy: the belief is that unions will not do something, no one ever attempts to do it, it does not get done, and the unions are blamed. Our experience and research show that enough school staff members are eager and willing to do what needs doing to make the schools productive and rewarding places to work. But those members are held back by procedures and traditions, including the self-fulfilling mythology about unions. Many schools are already doing everything that is suggested here (see Pinnell and others, 1981, and Wayson and others, 1982). Their staff members engage in role enrichment activities when:

• they see the personal and professional value;

• the activities are voluntary and spring from the person's own decisions;

• members have felt the personal reward of being able to use their own skills to control their own fate; and

• they see the personal advantage of being able to work in a more positive situation with fewer discipline problems and less intrastaff conflict.

Improvement in school programs is blocked more by lack of ability at all levels of the profession to lead such endeavors than by opposition from unions.

Objective 3: To increase and widen students' sense of belonging in the school.

As students feel supported and are involved in the fate of the school, fewer disruptions or irresponsible behaviors will occur. Just as staff members need to feel a greater sense of personal responsibility for the school, the same is true of students to an even greater degree. The more the students feel the school is theirs and the more pride they have in being part of the school, the easier will be the staff's job. The Phi Delta Kappa national survey of exemplary schools revealed that a large number had a very active student participation in the life of the school (Wayson, 1982). In schools that have a high degree of student belongingness:

- Less graffiti, litter, and vandalism are evident.
- Students play a highly responsible role in service projects, such as school beautification.
- Students are involved in rule making, assessment, and implementation.
- Teachers always seem human; therefore, they are not always right.
- Student leaders are recognized as part of the organization and are significantly involved in decision making.
- T-shirts, buttons, flags, signs, and the like express school spirit and a feeling of pride.
- There is high student participation in extracurricular activities, even on the part of students who do not live in the immediate school neighborhood.
- Students play service roles in various areas of the school such as the office and the cafeteria.
- Students plan and run activities such as assemblies.
- Staff members know students' names; staff and students call each other by name.

Supervisors and administrators often reduce students' involvement without knowing it. Policies and practices intended to improve student discipline can actually increase discipline problems. Decreasing student interaction, increasing security personnel,[5] increasing the number of rules, installing devices such as metal detectors, and locking classroom doors all reinforce the idea that the school is a dangerous and foreign place for students. Such practices make the school feel more like a prison than a place where students belong. While such measures may be temporarily useful in some schools, their use should be carefully weighed against the consequences. Centrally created school codes of conduct can be so negative, so punitive, or so poorly introduced that they worsen the problems they are designed to overcome. Techniques that focus on punishment and rigid rule enforcement implemented without building the staff's understanding of the relationship between school discipline and other features of the school environment can also create an atmosphere that actually increases serious discipline problems. Such disciplinary programs can be effective when implemented in a context in which adults and students have built up good communication and relationships, and have used numerous other techniques to increase pride and belongingness.

---

[5] *Some* security personnel actually improve student belongingness in schools where they know more about student behavior than the instructional staff does.

Once staff development programs have been implemented to teach staff members skills in problem identification, brainstorming, reaching consensus, and action planning, those skills can be taught to students. For example, Mifflin Middle School in Columbus, Ohio, used simple action planning techniques to get students involved (see Urich and Batchelder, 1979). A group of students established goals, developed success indicators, designed activities, and designated responsible persons as a prelude to the December dance. Previously, student participation in such activities had been very low. All activities were completed, the list of students involved in the work grew, and the dance was well attended by both black and white students, something that had not happened before in this newly desegregated school. Students met the next day to begin work on the Valentine Dance. Another staff development meeting was coordinated with a meeting for students. Both staff and students rated the school and compared their assessments as a way to share perceptions.

Objective 4: To define rules and disciplinary procedures in ways that teach and reward self-disciplined participation.

When rules are made by the people involved and when expectations are clearly understood, there are fewer transgressions. Often, a school staff has never really talked about the school rules, whether they are effective, and what is meant by enforcement of them. The more nearly rules are derived from principles of learning and understanding of normal human behavior, the more effective they are. School staffs must take the time to go through the long and tedious process of making, assessing, and developing plans for implementing schoolwide rules. They also need to plan strategies for teaching rules to students. In schools that give attention to developing better rules and procedures for enforcement:

• Rules are seen as standard operating procedures that describe "the way people act here" rather than a list of "thou shalt nots."

• Rules are used in a way that teaches new behaviors and develops self-discipline in students.

• Staff members enforce rules consistently and in a sensitive and sensible way.[6]

• Enforcement does not focus on punishment.

---

[6] Consistency does not necessarily mean doling out standard punishments in the same way to every individual, regardless of circumstances. That, in fact, may be quite an inconsistent way to deal with misbehavior. It does mean consistently focusing on getting the behavior implied by the rule and on teaching the desired behavior to each student the way the student learns best.

- Enforcement of a rule means "getting the behavior you want from the person who is to follow the rule."
- Rules and expectations are clearly defined and understood by those who enforce them and those who follow them.
- School staffs evaluate and revise rules at appropriate intervals.
- The total staff works as a team to enforce schoolwide rules and communicate expectations to students.

Rule making and implementation is something that administrators and supervisory personnel have not given much attention to in the past. Their own training typically does not include preparation for this kind of staff leadership. Often their leadership depends on outside "consultants" who are expected to provide magic answers. However, any school staff with some hard work and cooperation can improve discipline by eliminating organizational causes for disruption. Developing and teaching effective rules is a good place to focus attention. All staff must realize—and supervisors and administrators can lead them to this realization—that simply reading rules to students is not enough. Teaching methods must be formulated to teach rules and the behavior they imply to students. Curriculum specialists in every subject area can be of great help to school staffs by helping them teach self-discipline, which goes beyond reducing disruptive behavior and focuses on work habits and completion of tasks as well.

In *Child Management,* Donald and Judith Smith (1978) offer some advice for making and enforcing rules. From that volume we have identified and elaborated a set of "rules for rules," which include the following:[7]

1. Rules must be stated and taught in such a way that those affected by the rule can understand what behavior is expected.

2. Rules must be reasonable; they must be necessary and consistent with normal behavior for children, young people, or adults.

3. Rules must be enforceable; it is silly to waste staff energy enforcing a rule that would take more resources than are feasible.

4. Once a rule is made, enforce it every time until the new behavior is learned. Enforcement is not punishment; it is getting the behavior you want.

5. Ignore behavior not covered by the rule (distractions such as tears, or bursts of temper).

Those criteria can be effectively used in a staff inservice session designed to make better rules and more effective enforcement. Staff members can

---

[7] *Developing Schools That Teach Self-Discipline.* A Seminar Developed by Synergetic Development Inc., William W. Wayson, Director.

assess the school rules and boil down the list until it represents something they can effectively enforce. Several schools have found it helpful to select, through consensus, five or fewer "priority" rules that they will agree to work on together. They draw up action plans that include enforcement strategies and consistently assess their progress in enforcing a particular rule. The planning process gives strong school staff members a chance to give suggestions to those who are having difficulties. Since all are working to develop the list of implementation strategies, defensiveness is removed. The rule represents desirable behavior for students. When almost all students are exhibiting the behavior, the rule is no longer a "high priority" because it has become a part of the "way people behave in this school" and new priorities can be established. Another effective technique for helping school staffs become more responsible for rule implementation is to provide feedback, such as number and type of office referrals, number of suspensions by race and sex, attendance, and so on.

Objective 5: To enhance curriculum and instructional practices to emphasize learning.

The curriculum is the heart of the school experience. It must be seen as more than the content to be taught in subject matter classes. Broadly conceived concepts of curriculum with content and processes appropriate for students and with greater variety and diversity tend to reduce discipline problems within the school. Students who don't understand the content or how it fits into a whole picture are likely to be discipline problems. Students who are not challenged to do their best work are likely to be discipline problems. Students who have not learned to focus attention on a task and to complete the job are likely to be discipline problems. Not only do such factors cause problems for the teacher or staff member, poor work habits and lack of self-discipline can seriously affect the student's whole life. In a school with a challenging and well-defined curriculum:

- A variety of teaching styles are used to meet a variety of learning styles.

- Teachers individually diagnose students' strengths and needs and plan learning experiences accordingly.

- Curriculum is not "blindly" implemented as a series of rigid steps; it is adjusted to maximize individual learning.

- Teachers know why they use the methods they do.

- Teachers meet students "where they are" academically.

- Students are able to get individual help when they need it.

• Every teacher considers teaching desired behavior as part of the teaching role.

• Activities are planned to address directly the teaching of self-discipline.

• Lesson plans for content areas include plans for developing self-discipline among students.

• All areas of the school, even hallways and cafeterias, are seen as learning places and plans are developed for teaching students to use those areas appropriately.

• The school provides many experiences—field trips, assemblies, special guests and speakers, attendance at community events—that allow students to learn appropriate behavior in a variety of contexts while enriching the subject matter they are acquiring.

Supervisors and curriculum consultants can play a key role in helping a school staff develop a dynamic and challenging curriculum that meets the individual needs of students. Sometimes, though, while performing their roles, they unintentionally act in a manner that can be dysfunctional. When the curriculum is totally conceptualized by someone other than those who teach it, the teachers lose any personal sense of responsibility for student learning outcomes. "I followed the teaching manual exactly; it's not my fault they didn't learn" is not an uncommon statement from teachers who have received a set of methods without really understanding what they are doing or why they are doing it. A curriculum framework is essential, of course, and teachers should be involved in its creation so they can understand why, and how, they should implement it. In addition, they must be able to determine individual differences among students and adapt the curriculum in such a way that the students are able to learn. Supervisors can assist teachers by helping them learn how to assess teaching and learning styles and to know the relationship between the two.

Supervisors can also be dysfunctional when they do anything that encourages staff to simply "cover the material." Supervisors and administrators can help to create a climate where giving individual help to students is a necessary and expected part of the teaching role. They can work with the staff to find additional adults (either paid or volunteer) who can increase the amount of individual time provided to students. Rocky River High School in Rocky River, Ohio, selects only staff members who are able and willing to teach one outside activity in addition to their content areas. The school has a large number of extracurricular activities to encourage participation on the part of the students. Staff members have a chance to establish relationships with students outside the formal classroom and are seen as "real people" rather than "walking textbooks."

Supervisors and administrative personnel can help by creating a climate that supports a broad definition of the teachers' roles and of curriculum and instruction. Several big city junior high and high schools have broadened staff members' roles as a result of action planning to address factors related to school climate.[8] (Incidentally, those were also schools in which there was strong support for teachers' and other unions.) Because staff members selected their own goals and designed their own approaches to achieving those goals, they felt positive about some additional responsibilities and felt a sense of accomplishment when many of their problems were alleviated, making their jobs easier.

Supervisors and curriculum consultants sometimes are the source of dysfunction when they separate the teaching of content areas from education's full responsibilities such as teaching disciplined use of the content in real life. Supervisors can help staff members by examining each area of the curriculum to determine how the area can contribute to the development of self-discipline. Department level meetings could focus on improving behavior: objectives and plans could be developed just as they are for the content areas. Staff members who are experiencing success can share techniques and ideas with those who are having problems. Supervisors and curriculum experts can play a key role in helping a school staff see discipline as something to be taught, both by adapting content instruction so more students will grasp it and by creating a total school environment in which each student is valued and engaged.

Objective 6: To provide assistance for dealing with personal problems that affect participation in the life of the school.

Much disruptive behavior is misdirected frustration, anger, fear, guilt, worry, or other emotions springing from events that take place in other portions of staff members' or students' lives. If the person has some way to vent, ease, redirect, or eliminate those emotions, the discipline problem would never occur. Teachers who fear parents, or who are anxious about their ability to discipline a class, or who are experiencing problems in their love lives are more likely to have discipline problems than are teachers who do not have such problems or who have learned ways to deal with them. Similarly, students experience family problems, growing problems, financial problems, and interpersonal problems with peers and members of the opposite sex. If they have no assistance in dealing with those problems, they can become emotional "bombs" waiting to go off.

---

[8] Eight middle, junior, and senior high schools in Cleveland and Columbus worked with the Institute for Effective Integrated Education at the Ohio State University's College of Education to develop climates that teach self-discipline (see Pinnell and others, 1981).

Schools that recognize the value of defusing such bombs build in continuing attention to personal needs. In such schools:

- There is counseling for staff members.
- People have support groups to go to with their problems.
- Staff and students openly discuss emotions, personal problems, and techniques for dealing with human emotions.
- People admit mistakes and seek feedback to improve.
- Cultural differences are openly recognized with visible evidence that the differences are valued (Forehand and Ragosta, 1976).
- Administrators and staff members permit one another to make mistakes and to take risks as they seek feedback to improve.
- Students deal with personal problems in classroom discussions.
- People smile at one another and touch during conversations.
- People admit causing problems.
- People know how to deal with conflict and do not escalate small problems into large ones.
- Staff members take fewer "sick days" and pay greater attention to duties.
- Students are absent and tardy less often and have fewer nondescript ailments.
- People experience negative stress and greater growth from positive stress.
- Emotional outbursts, gossip, or other misdirected efforts are fewer.

School systems, just like other organizations, have built-in forces that work against personal contacts. Organizations (including schools) treat people like pieces of equipment. Human needs and emotions are seen as deterrents to good organization. Administrative and supervisory personnel are constantly faced with the dilemma of getting the work done most quickly and efficiently while at the same time recognizing the human needs of the staff and the students. As school districts have grown in size and the stresses of modern life have increased, pressures have also increased to make schools less humane. Staffs are isolated from one another, and role specialization and centralized decision making have separated policies and practices further from the implementers. Personnel policies, which should give the employee *closer* contact with the organization, instead often accentuate the impersonal nature of the job. Misguided responses to legal decisions have made contacts more "businesslike" and less supportive and understanding. In large districts, supervisors may find that all of the communication with staff members is too much to do, and they fall back on impersonal and demoralizing memoranda, last minute meetings, poor follow-up, and form letters.

Administrators have supported the creation of huge "study" halls and the elimination of homerooms. Those practices have cut off some of the major personal ties that the student had with the school. Computerized grade cards and attendance systems have worsened already impersonal systems of contact. Staff are no longer on the playground or leading the after-school clubs; the personal contacts with students have been diminished if not eliminated. Open houses are drudgery for both staff and parents and do not facilitate close contact. Such practices lead to the type of depersonalization and the feeling of isolation and anomie that characterize much of modern society and lead to socially-disruptive behavior.

Administrators and supervisors can use their own relationships with staff members to model the types of behaviors that are needed throughout the school. They can remember names, use more personal types of communications, or organize teams or communication trees that give each person a human contact with the organization. They can also exhibit through evaluation systems and instructional improvement programs that they value individual teachers and students. They can demonstrate that they expect school personnel to contact students as individuals. Staff development can include all sorts of skills and techniques for dealing with human emotional problems, for recognizing symptoms of stress and anger, for dealing with frustration, aggression, and conflict.

Ironically, training that expands the staff members' responsibilities and gives them more importance can reduce stress and isolation more than eliminating duties and reducing the importance of the job. The following activities are being used in some school districts.

• Schools have created advisory systems in which staff members hold responsibility for knowing students and their families and linking them to the school.

• Schools have purposely expanded extracurricular activities to give every student a way of contributing to and participating in the life of the school.

• Districts have set up counseling centers that provide help for staff in such areas as drug and alcohol abuse, divorce, and job stress.

• Schools have established counseling discussions that use transactional analysis, reality therapy, or other techniques for helping staff members solve personal problems.

• Districts are providing retraining opportunities for people who may be laid off as the school population declines.

• Supervisors are trained to use helping relationship techniques in their work with school staff members.

• Staff development has been directed toward effective homeroom, study hall, and tutorial techniques.

Objective 7: To strengthen interaction between the school and the homes and community it serves.

Generally, more open transactions with parents and other community members result in better opportunity to improve achievement and behavior within the school. When teachers and other staff members communicate constantly with parents and the communication is of high quality, there is less chance for students to "play games" by using one against the other. In addition, of course, there are more adults who understand the students' problems and who try to be of help. It is important to point out that the majority of those communications must be positive. If almost all communications are negative, parents may not be as supportive of the school. If the school staff has first established trust, it is easier to talk to parents about their children's misbehavior.

Schools in the Phi Delta Kappa study reported constant communication wtih parents through newsletters, home visits, parent nights, grandparent days, and use of parent volunteers and other strategies (Wayson and others, 1982). Phi Delta Kappa schools also reported close and unusual relationships not only with parents but with the community served by the school. Community agencies were used to contribute to school life; school staff members were active in the community. At one school, a group of parents were trained as a "speakers bureau" to make presentations about the school to local service clubs.

It is important to note that the traditional "neighborhood school" concept is not necesary for those close relationships to develop. Schools form their own community with the people, businesses, and agencies with whom they interact. Many schools with a wide geographic population have strong feelings of community.

In a school that has strong relationships with the parents and community:

• Many volunteers, both parents and others from the community, are seen frequently in the school.

• Teachers and other staff members run meetings to help parents understand the school program.

• Teachers, students, and other school personnel give presentations about the school.

• Sometimes school meetings and other events are held outside the school in places in the community that are more convenient for parents who do not live near the school.

- School staff members have been in the neighborhoods where students live; they know the street names and gathering places.
- Community leaders are aware of the school and its programs; they consider the school a vital part of the community.
- Staff members have visited students' homes.

Supervisors, administrators, and specialists often act in ways that prevent teachers from attaining close relationships with parents or community agencies, and school staff members often expect them to do so. Most meetings with parents and most regular communications are typically conducted by school administrators or specialists such as counselors or parent/community agents. Just having such specialists tends to remove the expectation that all staff members will seek contact with parents and community. Specialists try to take over and do the job themselves. Instead, those persons should assist the staff in planning for and implementing a widespread communication network that can create a good public image and garner resources for the school.

Supervisors, administrators, and specialists also tend to act as intermediaries between parents and staff. Doing so deprives teachers of chances for developing leadership skills and confidence by running the meetings and making presentations themselves.

Too few supervisors reinforce the advantages of close home-school ties. Some actually work against them. A few, distrustful that teachers will represent the school well, forbid teachers to make direct contact and interpose themselves between the staff and the community.

Teachers may be fearful of contact with parents. They need support and confidence-building activities. Supervisors and administrators can be of great help in those areas; they can teach communication skills to school staffs and assist individuals to feel more comfortable with parents. At one newly formed middle school, seventh- and eighth-grade teachers had never had an individual parent conference day and felt apprehensive about the coming experience. During a staff-led inservice meeting, the sixth-grade teachers, who had had extensive experience, talked with the upper grade teachers about conferences, demonstrated a parent conference (with real parents), then assisted the upper grade teachers to practice conferencing. After the meeting, all staff members felt much more confident and parent conference day was a big success. Such experiences can be facilitated by supervisors.

A school staff that has had limited parent/community involvement needs to recognize that many staff members may feel apprenhensive in the beginning stages. Complaints about extra work often mask simple shyness or lack of confidence. We have found that a staff needs a series of experiences to gradually build their confidence and skills. For instance:

1. The staff can engage in team-building activities such as the camping expedition described earlier, so that they trust each other and are not afraid to admit anxiety and ask for help.

2. A "neighborhood walk" is a good beginning activity. School staff members go in small groups through the neighborhoods where their students live, preferably those neighborhoods with which staff are least familiar. They make a map of a three-to five-block area that indicates significant gathering places for the neighborhood. They interview three people on the street to learn what the community would like to see in the school. After the experience, they share what they have found.

3. Another session is devoted to making home visits. After hearing some simple guidelines, staff members make a home visit; those who lack confidence may ask another staff member to go with them. Afterwards they discuss their experiences.

4. Most meetings with parents are a "show" where parents listen to school personnel or watch presentations. Parents can successfully be involved in the same kinds of workshops that teachers use to brainstorm ideas and make action plans for improving the school. The goal of such meetings would be to build commitment on the part of parents. Any such meeting, however, must have a follow-up and the activity must not be dropped. Once parents indicate their willingness to help the school, they must be given a task; otherwise, it is hard to get them involved again.

Objective 8: To improve the physical appearance and the organizational structure of the school.

The more the school environment looks like a workshop, a library, a restaurant, or a conference center and the less like a prison or institution, the fewer discipline problems. The setting in which school activities take place should be generally pleasant, and provide convenient places for adults and students to work. It should also reflect the interests, culture, values, and activities of the students. From the very moment one enters the door, the building itself must communicate that "this is a place where people feel they belong, where they have pride, and where they work and achieve success." School staffs should constantly analyze the school environment and be aware of what students are learning from the school setting itself. In schools where staffs pay attention to the physical environment and organization:

• Personal contributions by students and staff are evident in the surroundings; for example, homemade curtains or student art is used in decorations.

• The school is decorated and inviting on the first day when students enter.

• Visitors see evidence that students are producing; for example, student work is carefully displayed in hallways, libraries, cafeterias, and classrooms.

• Students are involved in projects to improve the school environment; for example, beautification projects and planting days are high points of the school year.

• Bulletin boards are used to communicate information about the school to the whole community; for example, attendance charts may be publicly displayed.

• Littering is minimal, even at the end of the day.

• One sees little evidence of vandalism and graffiti.

• Repairs are made immediately so that the physical facility is in good shape.

• Parents are advocates for getting help to improve the school facility.

• Schedules and room assignments are used to achieve the objectives listed in this chapter rather than working against them.

Even an old building can be made to look inviting. At A. B. Hart Junior High School in Cleveland, the cafeteria was a big problem. It was an old facility with dark unfinished floors and not much light. Students and staff made red checkered curtains for the windows; the biology department raised plants and hung them all around the room; the art students covered one large wall with a mural depicting the history of the the school; a group of students made table and wall decorations. On special occasions, the home economics department put out tablecloths and centerpieces for some 1,000 students who ate in five shifts. The cooperative effort brought people closer together and made them feel successful. Another dramatic example comes from Franklin School in Newark, New Jersey. Staff, students and parents were so bothered by the condition of the building that they bought paint and redecorated the entire building. Now a school that was covered with graffiti has none.

Supervisors and administrators have a tendency to feel they can do nothing about the physical environment of the school or that it has nothing to do with their jobs. Inservice activities often concentrate on improving the transmission of content or alleviating discipline problems with little regard for the use of the physical space. For example, a number of fights may be occurring in one area of the building. A typical response would be to send more supervisors into that area or to enact more severe punishments for those who are fighting. It might be that the area is simply a "traffic jam" where a large number of students are trying to move quickly through the same space at the same time, leading to bumping, shoving, and fights. In a case like that, it is more beneficial to reroute traffic or change schedules than it is to increase controls, which may cause more problems than they alleviate. Similarly, cafeteria or study hall problems come about because those areas look and operate like a Jimmy Cagney prison scene. Supervisors, and specialists can help staff members by:

1. Teaching them to analyze problems in various areas of the building so that trouble spots can be pinpointed.

2. Examining policies, organizational patterns, schedules and other routine administrative decisions for their potential for fostering good or poor behavior. (For example, lunch schedules for both staff and students may unintentionally be created in such a way that some groups never get to communicate with each other, thus forming barriers that can lead to dysfunction in the organization.)

3. Encouraging staff members to use their planning skills to create a pleasant learning environment.

4. Encouraging the creation of visible signs that tell students they are welcome and belong in the school.

5. Promoting multicultural education workshops that teach staff members how to include minority students in all areas of the school, including displays, books, and programs.

6. Using their influence to assure that physical facilities are not permitted to deteriorate even when funds are scarce.

Summary

Reducing discipline problems is really a curricular problem requiring school personnel to place self-discipline at the top of the list of goals for schooling and to adopt methods for teaching the behaviors that are desired. Many discipline problems are traceable to common practices in organizing and operating schools, and modifying those practices will have more effect on school discipline than traditional methods of punishing or treating students as the cause. We have discussed eight features of schools that affect both staff and students' behavior. Those features combine to create a school community whose norms are the most powerful determinant of how people behave in the school. Modifying those features not only improves discipline but yields gains in achievement, staff and student morale, and community respect for the school. Attempts to make permanent improvements in discipline will fail if they do not deal with those eight features.

References

Combs, Arthur W., ed. *Perceiving, Behaving, Becoming: A New Focus.* Washington, D.C.: Association for Supervision and Curriculum Development, 1962.

First, John McCarty, and Mizell, M. Hayes, eds. *Everybody's Business: A Book About School Discipline.* Columbia, S.C.: Southeastern Public Education Program, 1980.

Forehand, Garlie A., and Ragosta, Marjorie. *A Handbook for Integrated Schooling.* Washington, D.C.: U.S. Department of Health, Education and Welfare, Office of Education, Office of Planning, Budgeting, and Evaluation, 1976.

Kaeser, Susan C. *Orderly Schools That Serve All Children: A Review of Successful Schools in Ohio.* Cleveland: Citizens' Council for Ohio Schools, 1979.

Lewin, K. *Field Theory in the Social Services.* New York: Harper & Row, 1956.

Pinnell, G. S., and others. "Final Report: An Institute to Develop Self Discipline in Newly Desegregated Junior High and Middle Schools in Cleveland and Columbus, Ohio." Washington, D.C.: U.S. Department of Education, 1981.

Pinnell, G. S., and others. *Directory of Schools Reported to Have Exemplary Discipline.* Bloomington, Ind.: Phi Delta Kappa International, 1982.

Schmuck, Richard A., and Runkel, Phillip J. *The Second Handbook of Organization Development in Schools.* Palo Alto, Calif.: Mayfield Publishing Company, 1977.

Smith, Donald, and Smith, Judith. *Child Management: A Program for Parents and Teachers.* Champaign, Ill.: Research Press, Inc., 1978.

Urich, T., and Batchelder, R. "Turning an Urban High School Around." *Phi Delta Kappan* 61 (November 1979): 206-209.

U.S. Department of Health, Education and Welfare. *Violent Schools—Safe Schools.* Washington, D.C.: U.S. Government Printing Office, 1978.

Wayson, W. W., and others. "A Handbook for Developing Schools with Good Discipline." Bloomington, Ind.: Report of the Phi Delta Kappa Commission on School Discipline, 1982.

Bibliography

American Friends Service Committee. *Creative Discipline: Searching for the Better Way.* Newsletter Series. Columbia, S.C.: Southeastern Public Education Program, 1977.

Brodinsky, Ben. *Student Discipline: Problems and Solutions.* Arlington, Va.: American Association of School Administrators, 1980.

Brophy, Jere, and Good, Thomas. *Teacher-Student Relationships: Causes and Consequences.* New York: Holt, Rinehart and Winston, 1974.

Brundage, Diane, ed. *The Journalism Research Fellows Report: What Makes an Effective School?* Washington, D.C.: The George Washington University, Institute for Educational Leadership, 1980.

Children's Defense Fund. *School Suspensions—Are They Helping Children?* A report prepared by the Children's Defense Fund of the Washington Research Project, Inc. Cambridge, Mass.: 1975.

Coles, Robert. *Children of Crisis: A Study of Courage and Fear.* Boston: Little, Brown, 1967.

Core Curriculum in Preventing and Reducing School Violence and Vandalism. Course 2: Discipline; and Course 3: School Climate. National School Resource Network. Washington, D.C.: Center for Human Services, 1980.

Cruickshank, Donald R., and others. *Teaching is Tough.* Englewood Cliffs, N.J.: Prentice-Hall, 1980.

"Developing Schools That Teach Self Discipline." Seminar developed by Professional Development Associates, William W. Wayson, Director. 2569 Sonata Drive, Columbus, Ohio: PDA, 1980.

Dreikurs, Rudolf, and Cassel, Pearl. *Discipline Without Tears*. New York: Hawthorne Books, 1974.

Ernest, Ken. *Games Students Play*. Millbrae, Calif.: Celestial Arts, 1972.

First, John McCarty, and Mizell, Hayes M., eds. *Everybody's Business: A Book About School Discipline*. Columbia, S.C.: Southeastern Public Education Program, 1980.

Foster, Herbert L. *Ribbin', Jivin' and Playin' the Dozens*. Cambridge, Mass.: Ballinger Publishing Co., 1974.

Ginott, Haim. *Teacher and Child*. New York: Avon Books, 1972.

Glasser, William. *Schools Without Failure*. New York: Harper and Row, 1969.

Gnagey, William J. *Motivating Classroom Discipline*. New York: McMillan, 1981.

Gordon, Thomas, and Burch, Joel. *T.E.T.—Teacher Effectiveness Training*. New York: Peter H. Wyden Books, 1974.

Howard, Eugene R. *School Discipline Desk Book*. New York: Parker, 1978.

Jersild, Arthur F. *When Teachers Face Themselves*. New York: Teachers College, Columbia University, 1955.

Jessup, Michael H., and Kiley, Margaret. *Discipline: Positive Attitudes for Learning*. Englewood Cliffs, N.J.: Prentice-Hall, 1971.

Jones, Vernon F., and Jones, Louise S. *Responsible Classroom Discipline: Creating Positive Learning Environments and Solving Problems*. Boston: Allyn and Bacon, Inc., 1981.

Kaeser, Susan C. *Orderly Schools That Serve All Children: A Review of Successful Schools in Ohio*. Cleveland: Citizens' Council for Ohio Schools, 1979.

Knoblock, Peter, and Goldstein, Arnold P. *The Lonely Teacher*. Boston: Allyn and Bacon, 1971.

Kounin, Jacob A. *Discipline and Group Management in Classrooms*. New York: Holt, Rinehart and Winston, 1970.

Lewin, Kurt; Lippitt, Ronald; and White, Robert K. "Patterns of Aggressive Behavior in Experimentally Created Social Climates." *Journal of Social Psychology* 10 (May 1939): 271-299.

North Carolina Department of Public Instruction. *Discipline in Schools: A Sourcebook*. Charlotte: Department of Public Instruction, 1977.

Combs, Arthur W., ed. *Perceiving, Behaving, Becoming: A New Focus*. Washington, D.C.: Association for Supervision and Curriculum Development, 1962 (chapter 6).

Phi Delta Kappa. "Study of Exemplary Urban Elementary Schools: Why Do Some Urban Schools Succeed?" Bloomington, Ind.: Phi Delta Kappa, 1980.

Pinnell, Gay Su, and others. *Directory of Schools Reported to Have Exemplary Discipline*. Bloomington, Ind.: Phi Delta Kappa, 1982.

Raths, Louis. *Meeting the Needs of Children: Creating Trust and Security*. Columbus, Ohio: Charles Merrill, 1972.

Robert, Marc. *Loneliness in the Schools*. Niles, Ill.: Argus Communications, 1973.

Rosenthal, Robert, and Jacobson, Leonore. *Pygmalion in the Classroom*. New York: Holt, Rinehart and Winston, Inc., 1968.

Sarason, Seymour B. *The Culture of the School and the Problem of Change*. Boston: Allyn and Bacon, 1971.

Schmuck, Richard and Patricia. *Group Process in the Classroom*. Dubuque, Iowa: William C. Brown, 1971.

Sheviakov, George, and Redl, Fritz. *Discipline for Today's Children and Youth*. Rev. ed. Washington, D.C.: Association for Supervision and Curriculum Development, 1956.

Smith, Donald and Judith. *Child Management—A Program for Parents and Teachers*. Champaign, Ill.: Research Press, Inc., 1978.

Wayson, William, and others. *Handbook for Developing Schools with Good Discipline*. Bloomington, Ind.: Phi Delta Kappa, 1982.

Wayson, W. W., and Pinnell, G. S. "Developing Discipline with Quality Schools." In *Citizen Guide to Quality Education*. Report of the Citizens' Council for Ohio Schools, Cleveland, Ohio, 1978 (pp. 1-26).

Wolfgang, Charles H., and Glickman, Carl D. *Solving Discipline Problems: Strategies for Classroom Teachers*. Boston: Allyn and Bacon, Inc., 1980.

Wynne, Edward. *Looking At Schools: Good, Bad, and Indifferent*. Lexington, Mass.: Lexington Books, 1980.

8

Are Public Schools Organized to Minimize Behavior Problems?

Daniel L. Duke and William Seidman

SOME individuals may argue that the question posed in the title is misleading. The contention might be that public schools are designed to provide various forms of instruction, not to control behavior. As a result, expecting schools to be organized to minimize the likelihood that student behavior problems occur would be judged unreasonable.

Such a claim ignores the widely recognized fact that schools exist for more than one purpose. Social control is clearly a major expectation of the public schools (Ianni, 1978). Students are supposed to be socialized into the norms of the adult world, learning how to behave appropriately in organized settings. In this chapter we explore the relationships between how students behave in school and the organizational characteristics of the school itself. We entertain the possibility that the ways schools are organized influence student behavior. The implications of such a possibility are great, given current concern over student disobedience, criminal conduct, and lack of motivation to work. Conceivably these dysfunctional behaviors can be lessened by altering school organization, rather than by attempting the difficult and frequently counter-productive task of changing students directly.

Assumptions About Schools as Organizations

Schools, like other complex organizations, are established to accomplish a variety of objectives. Having said this, it is important to add that consensus does not necessarily exist about what these objectives are or should be. Different schools strive for different objectives, and the objectives of particular schools change over time. Organization researchers hasten to

Research for this chapter was supported, in part, by the Teacher Corps.

point out that the stated or "public" objectives of schools may differ from the functions they actually serve (Katz and Kahn, 1978).

Despite these qualifying observations, it is reasonable to maintain that most schools are characterized by (1) a sense of what they are supposed or expected to accomplish, and (2) an organizational structure intended to facilitate the accomplishment of their objectives. It is unfair and unfortunate that much recent criticism of schools portrays educators as rudderless quasi-professionals uncertain about what to do and how to go about it. Such simplistic attacks overlook the difficulty educators encounter in dealing with conflicting sets of expectations, limited and uncertain budgets, and lack of public support.

Still, it would be a mistake to err in the opposite direction and believe that schools are organized to efficiently and completely accomplish all of their objectives as well as can be expected. The burgeoning ranks of management consultants and organization development specialists working with schools testify to the growing awareness that school organization may need to be modified in order to improve effectiveness. Researchers are devoting more attention to the relationship between school organization and school outcomes (Bridge and others, 1979; Centra and Potter, 1980; Clune, 1979; Duke, 1980).

To point out that work dealing with school organizational characteristics is increasing is not to say, however, that general agreement exists about terminology or what constitutes an organizational characteristic. Centra and Potter (1980) include in their list of "within school conditions" such factors as administration-teacher ratio, degree of control, reward mechanisms, tracking, teaming, peer influence, and class size. Bridge and others (1979) identify as "school inputs" the following: expenditure per pupil, ability tracking, school size, nonteaching staff, teacher turnover, teacher salaries, physical plant, age of school building, library and supplies, class size, and school calendar. Lists of factors such as these suggest considerable confusion about what constitutes an organizational characteristic.

For the purposes of this chapter, an organizational characteristic will be regarded as any dimension of organizational structure. Organizations—including schools—consist of objectives, processes, and structures (Kahn, 1977). Processes, primarily concerned with the production of goods or services, are directly related to the achievement of organization objectives. Structure encompasses those mechanisms that ensure organization processes can be carried out. Pugh (1969, p. 115) puts it thusly:

All organizations have to make provision for continuing activities directed towards the achievement of given aims. Regularities in such activities as task allocation, the exercise of authority, and coordination of functions are developed. Such regularities constitute the organization's structure. . . .

The following diagram illustrates the organization model used in this essay.

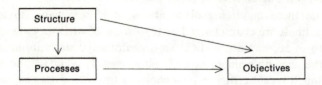

The vectors in the model suggest that the achievement of organization objectives is influenced by structural factors working directly on outcomes or through organization processes. What, specifically, are those structural factors, or, as they will be referred to subsequently, organizational characteristics? Some of the characteristics that may serve as independent variables for researchers studying school outcomes are arranged into the following five general categories:

    I. Unit structure
        A. School size
        B. Class size

   II. Task structure
        A. Division of labor
            1. Specialization
            2. Departmentalization
        B. Student grouping
            1. Ability grouping
            2. Cultural, ethnic, or racial grouping

  III. Resource allocation structure
        A. Allocation of time
        B. Allocation of space
        C. Allocation of materials and equipment

  IV. Authority structure
        A. Levels of authority
        B. Decision making mechanisms

    V. Control structure
        A. Rules
        B. Standards of performance
        C. Evaluation
        D. Supervision/coordination
        E. Rewards
        F. Sanctions

Unit structure pertains to the basic divisions of school organization or what some theorists term production units. The two units most often discussed by educational researchers are the school and the class.[1] The size (number of students) of these units can vary from school to school and depends on school policy as well as local enrollment. In other words, two school systems with the same student population may decide to establish different bases for school and class sizes. Unit size can influence other organizational characteristics as well as overall effectiveness.

Within organization units various tasks are undertaken in order to accomplish objectives. These tasks are distributed among various school employees, constituting a division of labor. Some employees, such as school psychologists, specialize in a relatively narrow range of tasks, while others, such as elementary teachers, are responsible for a wide range of tasks. Individuals with similar areas of specialization may, in turn, be grouped into departments. A few elementary and almost all secondary schools are departmentalized, but patterns of departmentalization vary across schools. Task structure encompasses groupings based on student characteristics as well as employee expertise. Ostensibly for instructional purposes, schools often group students on the basis of ability.[2] For other reasons, students also may be grouped according to cultural, ethnic, or racial characteristics.

In order to accomplish organization tasks, resources are needed. Money, of course, is the ultimate resource. Money buys other resources, including time (personnel), space (facilities), and materials. How these resources are to be allocated and for what purposes are organizational decisions that emerge from the school authority structure. Authority structure is characterized by various levels, ranging from the superintendent and central office administrators to building principals, department chairpersons, and teachers. Larger school systems tend to have more levels of authority. Decision making occurs at each level, though the mechanisms for making decisions and the individuals involved vary.

To ensure that all other organization structures function smoothly, control structure exists. Using a variety of control mechanisms, including rules, standards of performance, evaluation, supervision, rewards, and sanctions, schools try to maximize the likelihood that their objectives will be achieved.

The preceding list of structures and characteristics is not intended

---

[1] Schools can be regarded as units when the school district is considered to be the "organization" in question.

[2] Some critics contend that the actual purpose of ability grouping is social control rather than instructional effectiveness.

to cover all dimensions of school organization. At best, they describe some of the more important landmarks encountered by students of school organization. Schools are presumed to vary along these dimensions. While considerable research has been done on the first three structures, authority and control structure have not been studied extensively, at least as they relate to school objectives.

School Objectives Related to Student Behavior

The point we are considering here is whether *organizational characteristics influence the ability of schools to accomplish certain objectives related to student behavior*. In selecting six sample objectives, we have made an attempt to be representative rather than comprehensive. We do not claim that all schools pursue each objective. It is likely, though, that most public elementary and secondary schools attempt to accomplish at least some of them.

The first objective is to maximize the likelihood that students obey school and classroom rules. This objective lies at the very heart of the issue of school discipline and classroom management, two major contemporary concerns for the public and the education profession. The remaining objectives can be related in one way or another to the first one. In other words, the accomplishment of each of these five objectives is considered by at least certain educators to be contingent on the willingness of students to obey rules. These objectives include:

1. Reduce student victimization.
2. Encourage students to cooperate with each other and develop good citizenship skills.
3. Enhance self-esteem.
4. Ensure the acquisition of "basic" skills.
5. Maximize the likelihood that all students will graduate.

The fact that none of the six objectives deals directly with teachers or other school personnel should not be interpreted as an indication that the welfare of these individuals is not of critical importance to the accomplishment of student-centered objectives. It is recognized that if teachers are victimized or if their self-esteem is disregarded, school effectiveness is likely to be adversely affected. Space limitations unfortunately prevent a detailed analysis of the relationship between organizational characteristics and teacher productivity.[3]

---

[3] Readers interested in this topic are referred to the forthcoming book by Daniel L. Duke, *Teaching—The Imperiled Profession*.

Rule-Governed Behavior

That students should learn to obey school and classroom rules has been one of the central expectations of most education systems. Various euphemisms have been coined to characterize the acquisition of rule-governed behavior: good citizenship, student accountability, respect for authority, responsibility, discipline. While traditionally the objective of rule-governed behavior was taken so much for granted that it rarely appeared in formal statements of school objectives, recent years have found more public acknowledgement by school officials that they are striving to promote good "discipline." To a great extent this action has been prompted by popular criticism of student conduct and what are perceived to be relaxed standards for behavior in school.

Beneath the groundswell of concern about rule-governed behavior lies considerable confusion and disagreement about what specific objectives schools should be pursuing. For example, take the matter of student responsibility. It can be expressed as an objective in at least two ways: (1) maximize the incidence of responsible student behavior, and (2) minimize the incidence of irresponsible student behavior. While the two objectives appear to be identical, in fact they can imply quite different organizational responses. To minimize irresponsible behavior, a school may eliminate opportunities for rule-breaking—in other words, remove sources of temptation. Thus, bathrooms can be equipped with recessed fixtures and grafitti-proof walls, teachers can be ordered to keep all materials under lock, and campus supervisors can prevent large groups of students from congregating.

None of these actions, however, is likely to encourage students to acquire or demonstrate responsible behavior. Students are less likely to learn responsibility by having all temptations to behave irresponsibly removed than by confronting opportunities to misbehave and choosing not to. To encourage responsible behavior, then, a school may need to teach it directly (or at least model conscientiousness), provide ample opportunities for students to exercise responsibility, and allow for the withdrawal of these opportunities when students act irresponsibly.

The remainder of this section focuses on what research says about developing responsible behavior. It should be noted though that many schools seem to place greater emphasis on the negatively-stated objective— the discouragement of irresponsibility.

As far as the present analysis is concerned, the central question for educators is, "Can school organization be altered in order to encourage greater rule-governed behavior?" One way to address this query is to consider the rules themselves. Three aspects of rules may be important: their nature, number, and consequences.

Ostensibly, rules—as components of the control structure—are designed to ensure that the school's purposes are realized. Those who regard the primary purposes of schools to be custodial in nature contend that rules typically become ends in themselves rather than means toward more academic outcomes (Duke, 1978b). Rules often seem to exist more for the convenience or protection of school employees than for the welfare of students.

Such a critique raises the possibility that the nature of the rules themselves may be related to how well students obey them. It may be that students have less respect for rules that do not seem to address their concerns (Duke, 1978a). One organizational strategy for increasing the acceptability or legitimacy of school and classroom rules is to involve students in determining the rules. McPartland and McDill (1976) review research on the role of school factors in the etiology of youthful crime and report that student involvement in school decision making has a measureable positive impact on attitudes opposing violence and vandalism. Field studies of 19 alternative high schools in California revealed extensive student involvement in decision making, and few behavior problems (Duke and Perry, 1978). The latter finding is all the more impressive because the alternative schools typically enrolled large numbers of students labeled as "behavior problems." Additional support for student involvement comes from case studies of 12 California high schools (Perry, 1980). Student involvement in school and classroom decision making distinguished schools with relatively few reported behavior problems from more troubled schools. Student involvement is a key component of many contemporary programs for increasing the effectiveness of classroom management. The programs include Assertive Discipline, Logical Consequences, Systematic Management Plan for School Discipline, and Teacher Effectiveness Training (Duke and Meckel, 1982).

The number, as well as the nature, of school and classroom rules may be related to student behavior. A typical response to perceived increases in misconduct over the past century has been to add more rules and make punishments more severe. The fact that misconduct has continued to increase over this period suggests that such a strategy may need to be reconsidered. Conceivably, for example, *fewer* rules could contribute to fewer behavior problems (Duke, 1980). This result may occur not only because certain behaviors once defined as unacceptable are redefined as acceptable, but also because the existence of large numbers of school and classroom rules taxes the capacity of school employees to enforce rules effectively, while still providing student services. The argument is that a lengthy list of poorly enforced rules invites more rule-breaking than a shorter list of consistently enforced rules.

The validity of this argument is rarely acknowledged by educational researchers. More often than not, they see inconsistent rule enforcement as a function of teacher differences. For example, three British researchers who studied school rules in a variety of settings posed their central problem thusly (Hargreaves and others, 1975, p. 37):

. . . should we conceptualize the variation in rule enforcement as a product of individual differences among teachers in their desire or capacity to enforce a set of classroom rules that are common to all teachers, or should we argue that under different teachers the classroom rules themselves differ?

While teacher differences obviously play a role in determining the extent to which students obey rules, it is likely that these differences are themselves subject to the influence of such organizational characteristics as the number of school rules.

Some support for the benefits of fewer rules comes from the previously cited study of alternative schools (Duke and Perry, 1978). Many of these schools functioned quite well with only two basic rules—one governing attendance, the other concerning respect for the rights of fellow students. It can be argued, of course, that these alternative schools could function effectively with few rules because of their small size. The average enrollment was 111 students. Organization theory does, in fact, predict that the extent to which rules are created to guide behavior (formalization) tends to increase as the size of the organization grows.

Reducing the number of rules may be less a strategy to encourage rule-governed behavior than to discourage irresponsible behavior. In other words, eliminating rules may be interpreted as an example of removing temptation—the temptation to break a rule. The Danes claim, for example, that removing laws forbidding pornography has resulted in decreased sex-related problems. It is unclear, however, whether or not the Danes presently consume more pornography than in pre-legalization days.

Rule reduction also can be viewed as representing more than a strategy intended to reduce irresponsible behavior. The presence of few rules may communicate to students that they are expected to function responsibly without lots of external constraints.

To investigate whether or not students resent the imposition of too many rules—along with other dimensions of bureaucratization—Anderson (1973) designed a study to measure alienation and perceptions of bureaucracy among high school students. The alienation instrument included Likert-type items covering five dimensions of alienation: powerlessness, meaninglessness, misfeasance, futility, and self-estrangement. Data were collected from all sophomores in 18 randomly selected Ontario, Canada, high schools. School bureaucratization was found to explain less than 5 percent of the variance in alienation from school. Still, Anderson contends that organizational characteristics should not be considered trivial. He argues that school organization is influential, but that it probably influences students in the same school in different ways.

Other organizational characteristics, such as rule enforcement procedures, may be related to rule-governed behavior as well. California's Task Force on the Resolution of Conflict conducted interviews in 32 high schools to gather perceptions of the causes of problems. They heard students identify a number of factors related to rule enforcement, as well as the rules themselves (California State Department of Education, 1973, p. 9):

1. Uneven application of discipline by the school staff and favoritism toward "student government cliques"
2. School smoking regulations
3. Unfair and authoritarian administration practices
4. Poor counseling services
5. Lack of a student role in the decision-making process
6. Tracking
7. Oppressive school policies (suspension, clothing codes, and so forth)
8. Discrimination against low-income students through the assessment of fees for participation in school activities

When teachers, counselors, and administrators were asked the same set of questions, they provided an entirely different list of causes, including excessive administrative paperwork, poor facilities, and home values.

Is there some validity to student perceptions of the etiology of school conflict? To what extent have aspects of school control structure such as rewards and sanctions been shown by researchers to be related to rule-governed behavior by students?

Behavior modification advocates maintain that the likelihood of an individual learning an appropriate behavior is increased by rewarding either the behavior when it occurs or approximations to it. They observe that sanctioning inappropriate behavior may reduce the occurrence of the misconduct in the short-run, but that this tactic does little to teach individuals how they *should* behave. Thus, the extent to which school control structure reinforces rule-governed behavior rather than sanctions disobedience may influence the overall level of student behavior problems.

Another potentially relevant dimension of rule enforcement concerns the nature of the consequences for rule disobedience. Dreikurs, a psychoanalyst, contends that the presence of logical consequences for rule-breaking helps to reduce behavior problems (Dreikurs and Cassel, 1972). If one conceptualizes school rewards and sanctions as intentions—rewards intended to encourage appropriate behavior and sanctions to discourage inappropriate behavior—then it is important to determine whether students perceive rewards and sanctions as they are intended. The following matrix describes the possible perceptions.

		Perceptions	
		Costly	Beneficial
Intentions	Rewards	1	2
	Sanctions	3	4

From an organizational perspective, it is reasonable to expect rewards to be perceived as beneficial (2) and sanctions as costly (3). If, however, students perceive rewards as costly (1) or sanctions as beneficial(4), the rule enforcement process probably is not functioning effectively. Just this problem can arise when a school administrator suspends a chronic truant (Duke, 1980). Rather than a sanction, suspending a student who illegally misses school often serves as a reward! Greater care in the design of consequences for both rule obedience and rule breaking seems essential if rule-governed behavior is to be encouraged.

Duke and Meckel (1980c) identify five organizational characteristics that contributed to the ineffectiveness of efforts in two urban secondary schools to deal with illegal absenteeism. A year's field work in the two schools led the researchers to note that various attempts to reduce student truancy had failed. They speculated that basic characteristics of school organization might be undermining the success of such corrective strategies as detention hall for truants, greater teacher involvement in monitoring absenteeism, and campus patrols. These organizational characteristics included the division of labor, the problem definition process, how decisions were made regarding school rules, training and selection, and school control structure.

Observations and interviews in the two schools confirmed that problems with these aspects of school organization were likely contributors to continuing attendance problems. For example, two elements of division of labor—role confusion and coordination between role groups—fostered ineffectiveness. Both schools had experienced increases in the number of tasks related to handling attendance problems. Tasks encompassed setting attendance policies, enforcing them, keeping records on absences, validating student excuses, determining what to do with truants, monitoring detention hall, and notifying parents. As the number of tasks grew, so too did confusion over who was expected to do what. Little administrative attention was devoted to resolving these coordination problems. As a result, students sometimes were sent to detention halls too crowded to accommodate them, parents were not notified promptly when children were absent illegally, and attendance clerks were unavailable to process excuses when students had free time.

A second study that looked at the relationship between a variety of organizational characteristics and student behavior comes from England (Rutter and others, 1979). Researchers conducted fieldwork in twelve inner-London secondary schools for three years. Some of the schools registered much greater academic and disciplinary success than others. These differences could not be totally explained in terms of variations in the characteristics of students attending these schools. Rutter and his group collected data on various factors that might help account for outcome variance: physical features of the schools, administrative characteristics, school processes, and ecological influences. Among the aspects of school organization that correlated with higher student achievement and better behavior were the availability of incentives and rewards for students and the existence of opportunities for students to exercise responsibility (that is, student involvement in school decision making). Other organizational factors, such as school size, allocation of space, and sanctions for disobedience, were not related to outcomes. Interestingly, rules were not selected as an independent variable because they did not vary much across school sites. Thus schools with essentially similar rules governing student behavior may differ considerably in terms of achievement and behavior.

Though some organizational characteristics varied along with outcomes in the Rutter study, they were not as powerful indicators of success as were qualities of the school as a social institution. Particularly influential were factors such as degree of academic emphasis, teacher behavior during lessons, and quality of working conditions for students.[4] The cumulative effect on these factors was considerably greater than the effect of any individual factors on their own.

While *15,000 Hours* failed to find school size an important correlate of rule-governed behavior, other research suggests that the number of students a school enrolls may be relevant. Garbarino (1978, p. 164) reviewed a variety of studies of school size and concluded that, "Small schools emphasizing the creation and maintenance of enduring personal-

---

[4] Rutter and others considered rewards and punishments to be social institutional characteristics rather than organizational factors.

ized social networks among students and staff offer considerable promise for the prevention and control of school crime." McPartland and McDill (1976) reanalyzed data collected from 900 principals in 1965 by Coleman and report that school size was positively related to principals' reports of the extent and seriousness of student misconduct. While the relationship was small in terms of the total variance explained, it was significant. In addition, the analysis of the data controlled for student ability level, racial composition, and socioeconomic status. Thus, student body differences cannot be offered as the reason big schools tend to report more behavior problems. McPartland and McDill (1976, p. 19) speculate that

. . . all behavior is more visible in smaller schools and naturally subject to greater control. In small schools, where few individuals are anonymous, it is harder to avoid being recognized for possible misdeeds.

In a massive mail survey of 4,000 schools coupled with on-site surveys of 642 schools, researchers at the National Institute of Education found that smaller schools were less likely to be characterized by student violence. Still, they caution against placing too much blame on size (National Institute of Education, 1978, p. 132):

It is true that large schools have more property loss, but we should bear in mind that the larger buildings with more expensive equipment and more students provide more opportunity for loss. Actually, the per-capita property loss from large schools is not higher than in small schools.

School size may contribute directly to behavior problems, if it influences class size. Should larger schools tend to be characterized by greater teacher-student ratios, for example, a case can be made against them. The aforementioned Safe School Study found that schools are less disorderly when there are fewer students in each class and teachers teach fewer different students each week (National Institute of Education, 1978). These findings receive support from recent research on school retrenchment (Duke and Meckel, 1980b; Duke and others, 1981). Case studies of high schools where budget cuts have led to teacher firings and larger classes reveal increased difficulties with student behavior. The pattern seems to be the same: class size grows, teachers have less time to spend with each student, students become frustrated or bored, and behavior declines.

In summary, contemporary research provides qualified support for the contention that student rule-governed behavior is, in part, a function of how schools are organized. Consequently, educators faced with behavior problems are advised to consider various aspects of school control structure, including the nature and number of school rules, how rules are determined and by whom, provisions for rule enforcement, sanctions for disobedience, and rewards for appropriate behavior. Other organizational characteristics such as school and classroom size, division of labor, and coordination mechanisms may or may not influence student behavior.

It is also conceivable that organizational characteristics exert indirect influences on student behavior through their impact on the accomplishment of other school objectives. In the following sections consideration is given the notion that student behavior is a function of such factors as opportunity for victimization, cooperation among students, self-esteem, academic achievement, and progress toward graduation. To the extent that school organization affects these five areas, it can be said to influence student behavior indirectly.

Student Victimization

Communities are beginning to insist that schools be made safe for students to attend. The Safe School Study cites research indicating that teenagers are more likely to be victimized in school than elsewhere (National Institute of Education, 1978). Surveys of students indicate that during a typical month 11 out of every 100 had something stolen from them, 1.3 percent were attacked at school, and .05 percent were victims of extortion. One out of every five students said they feared being hurt or bothered at school.

A case currently pending in California against the Los Angeles school system claims that local schools are unsafe and thereby threaten to deprive students of equal access to an education—a basic right under the Fourteenth Amendment. Problems with truancy and poor work habits frequently can be traced to student fear. One type of behavior problem thus spawns other forms. As educators begin to think of the reduction of student victimization as a distinct objective for schools, they need to consider what role school organization may play in the etiology of the problem.

Among the eight clusters of recommendations presented in the Safe School Study and derived from principals, teachers, and students were several that concerned school organization. Firm and fair rule enforcement, careful monitoring and reporting of troublemakers, and student involvement in school decision making were all perceived to be critical in reducing student victimization. Support for better rule enforcement also comes from a recent conceptual piece (Duke, 1978b). It is speculated that school employees may display less zeal in handling problems arising between students than those between students and adults. Such a double standard, if it exists, can increase the likelihood of student victimization.

In a re-analysis of some of the Safe School Study data, Gottfredson and Daiger (1979) are able to extend the original findings to cover additional organizational characteristics. Student victimizations in 600 schools were related to teacher confusion over how school policies were determined (coordination) and how fair and clear school rules were perceived to be by students. Apparently, low levels of victimization are related to effective communications, both between administrators and teachers and between teachers and students. Interestingly, Gottfredson and Daiger also report that the more teachers indicated students should be involved in school decision making, the more students reported being victimized. This finding challenges the conclusion in the preceding section that student involvement is a key to rule-governed behavior.

Victimization also may be related to school grade-level organization. A comparison of six K-8 schools and eight K-6 schools in a mid-western city finds that students stood a significantly greater chance of being robbed or beaten in the former group (Blyth and others, 1978). The presence of older students—particularly males—in the K-8 schools apparently caused sixth graders to be subjected to more victimization than their counterparts in K-6 schools.

It is likely that most victimization occurs outside of class—before school, between classes, in cafeterias, after school, on buses, at special events (Duke, 1980; Metz, 1978). One organizational explanation for this tendency is that adult supervision generally is less well-provided outside of class. While altering grade-level organization may help reduce student victimization, it is unlikely the problem can be fully controlled without some provision for more thorough supervision of out-of-class areas and activities. Recent developments in the division of labor in schools find new roles being created to handle these extra-class supervisory duties (Duke and Meckel, 1980a). Many schools—especially urban secondary schools—currently employ door monitors to register all visitors, uniformed security guards, paraprofessionals serving as campus supervisors, bus supervisors, and student patrols. Increasing the number of role specializations requires more coordination by school administrators.

Cooperation Among Students

Certainly one way to reduce the likelihood that students will victimize each other is to encourage the development of cooperation among students. Cooperation entails putting aside personal interests to help ohers. As an objective of American public schools, however, cooperation tends to occupy an ambigious position. Teaching students how to compete often has rivalled in importance teaching them how to cooperate.

Very little research has been undertaken to learn more about the relationship between school organization and student cooperation. What research has been done typically has focused on teacher behavior and attitudes. It is reasonable, though, to expect the acquisition of cooperative skills by students to be influenced by certain organizational characteristics of schools, particularly size, rewards, and division of labor.

Though not an "organizational" study per se, Barker and Gump's *Big School, Small School* (1964) looks at the relationship between school size and a variety of student outcomes, including some proximal indicators of cooperation. For example, they report that small schools in their sample of 13 Midwest high schools were characterized by considerably greater levels of student participation in school activities. Despite the general presence of more opportunities to collaborate with peers in big schools, students in these schools did not take as great advantage of them as their small school counterparts. Big schools may unintentionally discourage student participation by minimizing the likelihood that a given student feels essential to the undertaking of an activity. Small school students may feel more indispensable.

Big schools seem to create climates more conducive to competition than cooperation. The presence of greater numbers of students means that students must compete more actively for teacher attention and recognition in general.

Aspects of school control and task structure, as well as size, also may influence cooperation. It was suggested in the preceding reference to *Big Schools, Small Schools* that student acquisition of cooperative skills might well be a function of the opportunities available to students to behave cooperatively. This proposition can be modified and extended thusly:

Student acquisition of cooperative skills is directly related to the availability to students of roles in which they are expected to cooperate and for which they are rewarded.

Some schools provide roles for students as cross-age and peer tutors, judges on student courts, and community service volunteers, but in general students have relatively few opportunities to demonstrate cooperation. When opportunities do exist, they rarely are accorded the status or recognition of competitive activities, such as sports and academics. How many schools, for example, actively seek to identify students who do the most for their school or community? If teaching students good citizenship is as prized as academic excellence, where are the valedictorians selected for achievement in the area of cooperation? The organization of most schools is likely to suggest to students that their sole responsibiliy is to do the best they can *for themselves.*

Self-Esteem

During the late 60s and early 70s considerable attention was focused on the affective needs of young people. How a person feels about himself was strongly linked—by professional judgment if not conclusive research findings—to academic achievement. Low self-esteem on the part of minority students and those from disadvantaged homes was offered as a primary cause for lack of success in school. While concern about self-esteem and affective development in general has been eclipsed by the back-to-basics movement, many schools still include references to them in formal statements of objectives. Does research say anything about the relationship between self-esteem and school organization?

To the extent that ability grouping or "tracking" is a function of school task structure, it can be argued that school organization influences student self-esteem. Tracking tends to reify class and status divisions, resulting in non-college preparatory students receiving less recognition and lower expectations. Stinchcombe (1964), in a case study of a predominantly middle-class high school, describes the obstacles faced by lower-class students. Contending that the "meaning" of the school experience derives from its symbolic value rather than tangible rewards, he claims that certain students—those destined for vocations—are prevented from identifying with symbols of success. As a result, they substitute adult symbols, such as cigarettes, cars, dating, and participation in extra-curricular activities. Stinchcombe concludes (1964, p. 132), "Adolescence comes to be undesirable to students whose future is not attractive enough to justify current subordination."

The negative effects of tracking on self-esteem may need to be modified in light of a recent study of heterogeneous and homogeneous grouping in Texas junior high schools (Sanford, 1980). Over the period of a year, an average of 14 observations were made in 52 mathematics and 50 English classes. Based on tests of student abilities, the classes were divided into heterogeneous and homogeneous samples and compared on a variety of measures. Of relevance to the issue of self-esteem is the finding that teachers in "extremely heterogeneous" classes may be less able to meet the affective needs of their students. They received lower ratings on such variables as listening skills, expression of feelings, receptivity to student input, and orientation to student needs. While tracking on the basis of career interests is not identical to within-class ability grouping, there are sufficient similarities in practice to suggest there may be optimal levels of mixed-ability grouping.

Barker and Gump (1964, p. 153) speculate that school size may be related to self-esteem. In a study of the effects of school consolidation, they report that small school students who were transferred to a large county high school were likely to experience a decrease in the "number of satisfactions associated with physical well-being, acquiring knowledge and developing intellectual interests, developing a self-concept, and zest for living."

In a review of research on the education of delinquents, Gold (1978) supports Barker and Gump's findings regarding school size. Interestingly, though, he challenges the previously mentioned notion that homogeneous grouping necessarily contributes to behavior problems. In the case of delinquent youth, Gold maintains that much of their behavior constitutes a psychological defense against threats to self-esteem. Smaller, more individualized programs—such as alternative schools for troubled students—often offer more success experiences and greater likelihood for productive teacher-student relationships, thus enhancing the development of self-esteem.

Besides school size and grouping practices, self-esteem may be related to grade-level organization. In the previously cited longitudinal study of K-6 and K-8 schools, seventh graders who were in K-8 schools grew continually more positive about themselves, while those who moved from a K-6 school to a junior high school felt less positive (Blyth and others, 1978). Their participation in activities dropped and feelings of anonymity increased.

Relatively little research has been done on the possible influence of other organizational characteristics on self-esteem. It is conceivable, however, that such factors as rewards, sanctions, opportunities for involvement in decision making, and responsible roles open to students may be related to how students feel about themselves. These feelings, in turn, would be likely to play a part in determining how students behave in school. Stinchcombe (1964) points out in this regard that young people who attend schools that do not value their aspirations tend to rebel.

Academic Achievement

One key element in the development of self-esteem can be academic success. Students who do poorly in their coursework not only tend to see themselves as failures, they often grow frustrated and resentful. Unable to keep pace with their peers, these students find school an unsatisfying experience. Frequently their discontent manifests itself in rule-breaking and rebelliousness (McPartland and McDill, 1976; Rutter and others, 1979; Stinchcombe, 1964). To what extent, then, is student achievement related to school organization?

How students are grouped by ability (homogeneous and heterogeneous) and aspirations (college preparatory, vocational, general) are two organizational characteristics that have been studied extensively. Overall, the results tend to be mixed.

In a comprehensive review of research on grouping practices, for example, Calfee and Brown (1979, p. 154) conclude,

The major finding with regard to the effects of ability grouping on outcomes for students (achievement, attitudes, and behavior) is that the low-ability student performs less well in school when placed with other low-ability students in homogeneous instructional groups, whereas the high-ability student, if influenced at all, benefits from assignment in homogeneous groups with other high-ability students.

Sanford (1980), on the other hand, reports that the achievement gains of lower ability junior high students tend to be lower in heterogeneous classes. Conceivably, then, there may exist optimal mixtures of students for different ability groups.

How instructional time is allocated is another organizational factor that has received considerable attention. In a review of the literature on school and teacher effects, Centra and Potter (1980) report that the amount of time teachers devote to direct instruction is directly related to student achievement. The question that has not yet been addressed by researchers, however, is "To what extent is the amount of time teachers allocate for direct instruction a function of school organization?" It is possible, for instance, that the nature of administrative supervision, how curricular decisions are made, and the number of non-instructional tasks assigned to teachers all influence how time in class is spent.

One of the few studies to look specifically at the relationship between school organization and student achievement focuses on a sample of 22 elementary schools participating in the third and final year of a national evaluation of the Emergency School Aid Act (Wellisch and others, 1978). Three "aspects of school management" were investigated: administrative leadership in instruction (supervision), coordination of instructional programs, and academic standards as evidenced through school policy regarding student promotion. Student achievement was based on gain scores on levels 2 and 3 of the California Achievement Tests. The sample was divided, using gain score data, into comparison groups—one group successful and the other unsuccessful in raising student achievement prior to the study.

Successful schools were found to be significantly more likely to be characterized by administrative leadership in instruction, coordinated instructional programs, and emphasis on academic standards. While the researchers found that administrators who were regarded as instructional leaders were associated with greater student achievement, they also note instructional policies were not made without teacher input. The key to effective leadership may be an ability to encourage broad-based involvement in decision making without abdicating administrative authority.

A final aspect of school organization that has been discussed—if not extensively researched—in relation to student achievement is control structure. Opinions vary, for example, as to the benefits of rewarding students for academic progress. Rutter and others (1979), report that various rewards—including teacher praise, displaying student work, and public recognition—are associated with student academic success. More immediate and direct rewards showed the strongest associations with student success. Amount of punishment displayed only weak associations with outcomes. Metz (1978) suggests that the effectiveness of positive reinforcement may vary according to student age. In her case study of two junior high schools, she observes that grades may not be as useful inducements in junior high as in senior high.

Graduation

An obvious objective for practically all schools is to graduate students, sending them along to the next level of learning or out into society. Whether or not students graduate is probably contingent, to some extent, on the accomplishment of most of the foregoing objectives. Students who disobey rules, are subjected to victimization, fail to cooperate with their peers, regard themselves with low self-esteem, and perform poorly in their courses are less likely to graduate than are their more successful cohorts. Has research, however, looked specifically at the relationship between school organization and the likelihood of graduating?

Considerable attention has centered on dropouts, but only recently have researchers considered the influence of school organization. The previously cited study by Duke and Meckel (1980c) concluded that organizational dysfunctions such as poor coordination of attendance policies contributed to the ineffectiveness of efforts by two secondary schools to monitor student absences—or what amounts to "benign neglect." Many students eventually drop out because they fall far behind in their work as a result of absenteeism. Evaluations of alternative schools suggest that these less formal organizations may be better able to "hold" certain students who are unable to adjust to conventional school rules and expectations (Duke and Muzio, 1978). Not all dropouts leave school because they dislike the constraints placed upon them, but it is likely that school control structure plays a supporting role in the etiology of many dropout problems.

Tracking may or may not influence dropout behavior, but it does seem to be closely associated with what students do after they graduate. Rosenbaum (1980), for instance, studied data from the National Longitudinal Survey of the High School Class of 1972. He reports that track placements are strong predictors of post-graduation activity. Rosenbaum also finds that student perception of track placement, a psychological factor, exerts an influence on post-graduation activity separate from actual track position.

Anderson and Tissier (1973) investigated the relationship between student aspirations and level of school bureaucratization. Selecting a stratified sample of 17 Ontario high schools with varying types of academic programs, they obtained questionnaire data from almost all tenth graders (3,605) in the schools. Possible aspirations included dropping out before graduation, completing high school and going to work, going on to a technical training course, and going on to a university. The measure of school bureaucratization consisted of 34 Likert-type items covering six separate dimensions: hierarchy of authority, rules, procedural specifications, impersonality, technical competency, and specialization. Like Stinchcombe (1964), Anderson and Tissier find that the type of program (track) in which a student is enrolled constitutes a major determinant of his aspirations. Strong confirmation of a link between aspirations and level of bureaucratization is not indicated, however.

Other Objectives

The preceding discussion encompasses only six school objectives. Obviously many more could have been selected. For example, nothing is said about possible relationships between school organization and creativity or equality of opportunity. No mention is made of teacher-related objectives, though it is reasonable to expect that efforts to make teachers feel better about their work will help in the accomplishment of student-related objectives. Objectives such as these are omitted largely because there is little or no relevant research to be found.

Researchers are encouraged to do more organizational studies of schools and school outcomes. Ideally, this research will not be based on the assumption that the only valid objectives to investigate are those concerning student academic achievement. It is the feeling of the authors, for example, that one of the most important potential objectives of schools is also one largely ignored by researchers—the creation of pleasant environments for young people. After all, whatever the preparatory and socializing functions of schools, students still must live seven hours a day for up to 13 years in them. Is it unreasonable to expect schools to be as comfortable and accommodating as possible? It may be that an important key to student motivation and productive behavior lies in the quality of school climate. School climate, in turn, may be closely related to school organization. At least these possibilities might be a good springboard for future research.

Conclusion

What response now can be given to the question posed as the title of this chapter? Are public schools organized to minimize behavior problems?

The small amount of relevant research yields mixed results. While few studies conclude that organizational factors are totally unrelated to student behavior problems, some find that these factors do not account for much of the between-school variance in student outcomes. Other studies find that factors such as tracking, rules, and rewards play a substantial role in determining how well schools accomplish objectives related to student behavior.

We believe that organizational characteristics can be extremely important influences on student behavior and that student behavior problems can be reduced, if not minimized, through organizational change. We have not cited more examples in the preceding pages because, in part, of the continuing preference of many educators to seek improvements through traditional channels—staff development, instructional redesign, curriculum development. The use of organizational development approaches in schools is still in its infancy.

To date, OD work has usually amounted to little more than "tinkering" with one or two organizational factors. It is likely that these piecemeal approaches to school improvement generally will fail to show dramatic results. The powerful inertial forces in many schools may only be overcome by comprehensive change—change in which schools are literally restructured. Such change is naturally more threatening and more costly, factors that probably explain why it has not occurred very frequently.

It would be well to investigate the handful of schools where comprehensive organizational change has been attempted. Such schools include alternative schools and Individually Guided Education (IGE) schools. Other studies could compare conventional public schools to private or parochial schools, which frequently are organized differently.

By conducting these types of studies, educators some day may be able to answer questions concerning the importance of school size, rules, decision making processes, resource allocation patterns, and other organizational factors. Are big schools better? What is the optimal level of supervision for students? How should teachers conceptualize their control functions? Are rules related to order? Without "hard" data to address these questions organizational change as an approach to reducing student behavior problems is less likely to attract educators' attention than conventional approaches stressing intervention on an individual or single classroom basis.

References

Anderson, Barry D. "School Bureaucratization and Alienation from High School." *Sociology of Education* 46 (Summer 1973): 315-334.

Anderson, Barry D., and Tissier, Ronald M. "Social Class, School Bureaucratization, and Educational Aspirations." *Educational Administration Quarterly* 9 (Spring 1973): 34-49.

Barker, Roger G., and Gump, Paul V. *Big School, Small School.* Stanford, Calif.: Stanford University Press, 1964.

Blyth, Dale A.; Simmons, Roberta G.; and Bush, Diane. "The Transition Into Early Adolescence: A Longitudinal Comparison of Youth in Two Educational Contexts." *Sociology of Education* 51 (July 1978): 149-162.

Bridge, R. Gary; Judd, Charles M.; and Moock, Peter R. *The Determinants of Educational Outcomes.* Cambridge, Mass.: Ballinger Publishing Company, 1979.

Calfee, Robert, and Brown, Roger. "Grouping Students for Instruction." In *Classroom Management,* the 78th Yearbook of the National Society for the Study of Education, Part II. Edited by Daniel L. Duke. Chicago: The University of Chicago Press, 1979.

California State Department of Education. "A Report on Conflict and Violence in California's High Schools." Sacramento: California State Department of Education, 1973.

Centra, John A., and Potter, David A. "School and Teacher Effects: An Interrelational Model." *Review of Educational Research* 50 (Summer 1980): 273-291.

Clune, William H. "Evaluating School Discipline Through Empirical Research." *Education and Urban Society* 11 (August 1979): 440-449.

Dreikurs, Rudolf, and Cassel, Pearl. *Discipline Without Tears.* 2nd ed. New York: Hawthorn Books, Inc., 1972.

Duke, Daniel L. "How Administrators View the Crisis in School Discipline." *Phi Delta Kappan* 59 (January 1978a): 325-330.

Duke, Daniel L. "Looking at the School as a Rule-Governed Organization." *Journal of Research and Development in Education* 11 (Summer 1978b): 116-126.

Duke, Daniel L. *Managing Student Behavior Problems.* New York: Teachers College Press, 1980.

Duke, Daniel L.; Cohen, Jon; and Herman, Roslyn. "Running Faster to Stay in Place: New York Schools Face Retrenchment." *Phi Delta Kappan* 63 (September 1981): 13-17.

Duke, Daniel L., and Meckel, Adrienne M. "Disciplinary Roles in American Schools." *British Journal of Teacher Education* 6 (January 1980a): 37-50.

Duke, Daniel L., and Meckel, Adrienne M. "The Slow Death of a Public High School." *Phi Delta Kappan* 61 (June 1980b): 674-677.

Duke, Daniel L., and Meckel, Adrienne M. "Student Attendance Problems and School Organization: A Case Study." *Urban Education* 15 (October 1980c): 325-357.

Duke, Daniel L., and Meckel, Adrienne M. *Teacher's Guide to Classroom Management.* New York: Random House, 1983.

Duke, Daniel L., and Muzio, Irene. "How Effective are Alternative Schools?— A Review of Recent Evaluations and Reports." *Teachers College Record* 79 (February 1978): 461-483.

Duke, Daniel L., and Perry, Cheryl. "Can Alternative Schools Succeed Where Benjamin Spock, Spiro Agnew, and B. F. Skinner Have Failed?" *Adolescence* 13 (Fall 1978): 375-392.

Garbarino, James. "The Human Ecology of School Crime: A Case for Small Schools." In *School Crime and Disruption*. Edited by Ernst Wenk and Nora Harlow. Davis, Calif.: Responsible Action, 1978.

Gold, Martin. "Scholastic Experiences, Self-Esteem, and Delinquent Behavior: A Theory for Alternative Schools." In *Theoretical Perspectives on School Crime, Vol. I.* Hackensack, N. J.: National Council on Crime and Delinquency, 1978.

Gottfredson, Gary D., and Daiger, Denise C. "Disruption in Six Hundred Schools." Report No. 289. Baltimore: Center for Social Organization of Schools, Johns Hopkins University, 1979.

Hargreaves, David H.; Hester, Stephen K.; and Mellor, Frank J. *Deviance in Classrooms.* London: Routledge & Kegan Paul, 1975.

Ianni, Francis A. J. "The Social Organization of the High School: School-Specific Aspect of School Crime." In *School Crime and Disruption*. Edited by Ernst Wenk and Nora Harlow. Davis, Calif.: Responsible Action, 1978.

Kahn, Robert L. "Organizational Effectiveness: An Overview." In *New Perspectives on Organizational Effectiveness*. Edited by Paul S. Goodman, Johannes M. Pennings, and Associates. San Francisco: Jossey-Bass Publishers, 1977.

Katz, Daniel, and Kahn, Robert L. *The Social Psychology of Organizations.* 2nd ed. New York: John Wiley and Sons, 1978.

McPartland, James M., and McDill, Edward L. "The Unique Role of Schools in the Causes of Youthful Crime." Report No. 216. Baltimore: Center for Social Organization of Schools, The Johns Hopkins University, 1976.

Metz, Mary Haywood. *Classrooms and Corridors.* Berkeley: University of California Press, 1978.

National Institute of Education. *Violent Schools—Safe Schools.* The Safe School Study Report to the Congress, Volume I. Washington, D.C.: National Institute of Education, 1978.

Perry, Cheryl L. "Adolescent Behavior and Criminogenic Conditions in and Around the High School." Ph.D. dissertation, Stanford University, 1980.

Pugh, D. S. "Modern Organizational Theory: A Psychological and Sociological Study." In *Organizations and Human Behavior*. Edited by Fred D. Carver and Thomas J. Sergiovanni. New York: McGraw-Hill Book Company, 1969.

Rosenbaum, James E. "Track Misperceptions and Frustrated College Plans: An Analysis of the Effects of Tracks and Track Perceptions in the National Longitudinal Study." *Sociology of Education* 53 (April 1980): 74-88.

Rutter, Michael; Maughan, Barbara; Mortimore, Peter; and Ouston, Janet. *Fifteen Thousand Hours.* Cambridge, Mass.: Harvard University Press, 1979.

Sanford, Julie P. "Comparison of Heterogeneous and Homogeneous Junior High Classes." Paper presented at the annual meeting of the American Educational Research Association, Boston, 1980.

Stinchcombe, Arthur L. *Rebellion in a High School.* Chicago: Quadrangle Books, 1964.

Wellisch, Jean B.; MacQueen, Anne H.; Carriere, Ronald A.; and Duck, Gary A. "School Management and Organization in Successful Schools." *Sociology of Education* 51 (July 1978): 211-226.

Authors

Jere Brophy is Professor of Teacher Education and Co-Director of the Institute for Research on Teaching, College of Education, Michigan State University, East Lansing.

Daniel L. Duke is Director, Educational Administration Program, Lewis and Clark College, Portland, Oregon.

Edmund T. Emmer is Research Scientist, Research and Development Center for Teacher Education, and Professor of Educational Psychology, The University of Texas, Austin.

Carolyn M. Evertson is an education consultant working from her home in Vandervoort, Arkansas.

Paul V. Gump is Professor, Department of Psychology, University of Kansas, Lawrence.

Vernon F. Jones is Associate Professor, Department of Education, Lewis and Clark College, Portland, Oregon.

Gay Su Pinnell is Program Director, Effective Integrated Education, Educational Foundations and Research, The Ohio State University, Columbus.

Mary M. Rohrkemper is Assistant Professor, Institute for Child Study, Department of Human Development, College of Education, University of Maryland, College Park.

Phil C. Robinson is Principal, Clarence B. Sabbath School, River Rouge, Michigan.

William Seidman is a doctoral student at Stanford University and Managing Director, Center for Cost Effectiveness Evaluation, Stanford, California.

William W. Wayson is Project Director, Effective Integrated Education, Educational Foundations and Research, The Ohio State University, Columbus.

Gail Von Huene is Program Specialist, Master Plan, Santa Clara County, California.